MW00535320

Wildflowers and the Call to the Altar

Wildflowers and the Call to the Altar

Mission and History of an Altar Society

SKYA ABBATE

Foreword by John C. Wester

RESOURCE *Publications* • Eugene, Oregon

WILDFLOWERS AND THE CALL TO THE ALTAR
Mission and History of an Altar Society

Resource Publications
An Imprint of Wipf and Stock Publishers
199 W. 8th Ave., Suite 3
Eugene, OR 97401

www.wipfandstock.com

PAPERBACK ISBN: 978-1-5326-6332-1
HARDCOVER ISBN: 978-1-5326-6333-8
EBOOK ISBN: 978-1-5326-6334-5

Manufactured in the U.S.A. NOVEMBER 12, 2018

In gratitude to the past members of the St. Francis Altar Society for their legacy of service.

To the present members of the St. Francis Altar Society for your legacy of faith.

To the future members of the St. Francis Altar Society for your discernment to answer the call to the altar.

"We are like a field of wildflowers growing together and made more beautiful by our diversity and differences, our fruits, our blossoms, and even our natural decline."

Skya Abbate, President, 2005–2018

Contents

Illustrations and Tables

Foreword

Our beautiful St. Francis Cathedral Basilica, nestled in the beautiful hills of Santa Fe, is a revered historical landmark that has given God honor and praise since it began almost 150 years ago. Home for the Catholics of the Santa Fe Archdiocese and a beacon for countless tourists, this sacred space serves as the mother church of the archdiocese where sacraments are celebrated, prayers are offered, and souls are nourished. Such a beautiful edifice requires incredible dedication and commitment on the part of many to ensure its vitality and its ability to meet the needs of God's people. Most of these good people work behind the scenes, quietly and selflessly, for the glory of God and the service of those who come to be refreshed and nourished at St. Francis Cathedral. Of these generous souls, none work harder and with more dedication than the members of the Cathedral Altar Society. I am grateful to Dr. Skya Abbate for shining a grateful light on these wonderful volunteers who give so much to the life of our mother church. For generations, the members of the Altar Society have ensured that all the appointments of the altar and worship space are of the highest quality and properly cared for, conscious of the part they play in the unfolding of the sacred mysteries. They do not ask for recognition or favor since they see their work as a service to God's people and a way of thanking God for all his blessings. Nonetheless, I am delighted to see the publication of Dr. Abbate's excellent and wonderfully crafted book that enables us all to deepen in our appreciation for those who serve at the cathedral altar behind the scenes but very much in front of our grateful gaze.

I thank Skya for her much needed book and I thank all the members of the Cathedral Altar Society for their unparalleled service and exemplary devotion to God and his Church. We Catholics firmly believe that the Lord Jesus Christ, who offered his life for us on the altar of the cross, became at once the priest and the sacrifice. The altar of St. Francis Cathedral stands as a sacred symbol of Christ and of his ultimate gift of love to us. *Wildflowers and the Call to the Altar, Mission and History of an Altar Society* reminds us that those who serve at the altar are serving Christ himself and the sacred mystery it represents. For this service, we in the Archdiocese of Santa Fe will be forever grateful.

Most Reverend John C. Wester
Archbishop of Santa Fe

Acknowledgements

In grateful acknowledgement to all those who helped make this book a reality

Copyeditor Elizabeth Grant

Translation of 1940 Spanish Altar Society By-Laws Angelina Gonzales Kollasch

Most especially thanks to the Spiritual Development and Writing Club Contributors who spent countless hours doing research, interviews, and proofing the book:

Skya Abbate is a Doctor of Oriental Medicine and college professor in New Mexico. She holds degrees in Sociology (MA), Pastoral Studies (MA), Bioethics and Health Policy (MA) and is a doctoral candidate in Catholic Bioethics and Health Policy. She has been the Altar Society President from 2005 to 2018, a member of the Liturgy Committee, the Pastoral Council, and the Sacred Heart League as well as an Extraordinary Minister of Holy Communion, Mass Coordinator, and Adult Altar Server. Her weekly articles on the liturgical year that she composed for the parish bulletin from 2004 to 2012 as the *Living Liturgy Series* were published in the book *The Catholic Imagination, Practical Theology for the Liturgical Year* (2012). She continues to write for the parish bulletin on select topics during Lent and Advent. She is the author of seventeen books within numerous genres.

Helen Anaya, a native of Santa Fe, graduated from St. Francis Cathedral School and Loretto Academy. She received her BA in Chemistry from the University of Mount St. Joseph in Cincinnati, Ohio. Following this she did a twelve-month internship at Penrose Hospital in Colorado Springs, Colorado in Medical Technology as a clinical laboratory scientist.

Tessie Anchondo is a native of Santa Fe. She is a life member of the Cathedral and attended St. Francis School as a child. She later graduated from Santa Fe High School in 1961. After graduation, she started her career with the U.S. Department of the Interior, Bureau of Land Management (BLM). Beginning as a stenographer and then as a secretary, she entered the field of adjudication which led to supervisory positions as unit chief and later as chief of the adjudication section, and then to lands and minerals, supervising one hundred employees in one of BLM's busiest offices. The bureau recognized Tessie in the form of several achievement awards, including the second highest department award, Interior Honor Award for Superior Service in 1990.

Yolanda Vigil Brewer, a native of Santa Fe, has recently retired from her position as Education Director at Zia Credit Union in Los Alamos and Espanola, New Mexico. She held this position for fourteen years. She has a Masters degree in Business Education and has fulfilled her life-long teaching career. She and her husband, Dan, have three children.

Margie Carrillo is retired from working in different offices, the last being a law firm where she was in the bookkeeping office and billing time for lawyers. She joined the Altar Society in 2006. She has served as the Secretary of the society for over eight years.

Roberta Quintana Gallegos is a lifetime member of the Cathedral Basilica of St. Francis of Assisi. In 2018, she would have been married for 60 years. Bobbie was blessed with five children, nine grandchildren, and a great grandson. Bobbie graduated from Loretto Academy and then attended the University of New Mexico as one of the first two military orphans to receive the G.I. Bill. She received her BS in Business Education in 1958 and retired from state government after 35 years of service. Her career included serving as a legal secretary/law clerk to Chief Justice M. E. Noble, as well as Justices Sisk, Oman, Compton and Stowers. She also served as Appointment Secretary to former Governor Jerry Apodaca. She retired in 1997 after serving as Administrative Assistant to Attorney General Tom Udall, now U.S. Senator. Bobbie considers her Catholic faith and education a great blessing. She has been a member of the Altar Society for over 35 years!

Olinda Garcia retired from state government and is currently a part-time administrative personal assistant. She has been a volunteer with the Chamber of Commerce for 20 years and honored as a volunteer of the year in 2006. She has been a volunteer at the Cathedral Gift Shop for over 14 years, a weekly collection counter for over 20, and Treasurer of the Altar Society for the last 18 years. She loves being with family and friends.

Leonor Anaya Mead, a native of Santa Fe, graduated from St. Francis Cathedral School and Loretto Academy. She received her BSN in Nursing from the University of Mount St. Joseph in Cincinnati, Ohio. She also did post-graduate studies in nursing cardiology from Mt. Sinai and Cedars of Lebanon Hospitals in Los Angeles, California. She was instrumental in establishing the first coronary care unit at St. Vincent Hospital Santa Fe, New Mexico. She served as the Altar Society President from 1999 – 2000.

Alice McKirnan, an Albuquerque native, attended Loretto Academy in Santa Fe for 12 years. Later, she moved to southern California and held various jobs with Travelers Insurance and James G. Wiley Import Export Company. She then worked in the dental field for over 20 years. During that time she married, had three children, six grandchildren, and one great grandchild. She retired after 40 years and returned to Santa Fe to care for her mother until her passing. She is a member of the St. Francis Altar Society and enjoys music, piano, gardening, spending time with family, and cooking.

Mary Jane Martinez was born and raised in Santa Fe, New Mexico and graduated from Santa Fe High School. She is the mother of five, grandmother of eight, and a great-grandmother of seven. She has held secretarial positions both in private and state agencies. She worked for the State Legislature for 27 years and held a secretarial position during Governor Jerry Apodaca's term in office. She served the Secretary of Region XIII National Association of Deacon Directors and as Secretary for the Policy Board of Deaconate Formation. She loves to spend time camping in the State and National forests. As a grandparent she spends a great deal of time attending school activities, sports, recitals and school plays. She served as the Altar Society President from 1995–1996.

Introduction

Altar Societies—Caretakers of the House of the Lord

It appears that a lesser-known ministry, the worthy story of Altar Societies, has been neglected in their important historical role in the Roman Catholic Church. Thus, their legacy, needs, and effects, which have endured to this day, are heralded in this little work. Altar Societies played, and continue to play, a vital role in the Catholic Church both by the physical care of the altar and through the cultivation of the spiritual growth of its members and the parish.

Historically, the primary mission of such societies was seen as an appropriate function to be carried out by women through their tending of the altar, linens, sanctuary, vestments, candles, and the provision of flowers. Some of this work was shared or assumed by sacristans in the past[1] and remains so even today. Yet, an important distinction about the work of these members is that it is more than housekeeping, albeit in the house of the Lord, but a veritable vocation that extends beyond the sanctuary into the divine milieu of community and creation.

Wildflowers and the Call to the Altar, Mission and History of an Altar Society is a fascinating story of the history of the St. Francis Altar Society embedded within the tri-cultural nexus of Santa Fe, New Mexico. Stemming from 1921 to the present the society responded to the call by Fr. Eligius Kunkel that the church, built in 1610, required a formal Altar Society to care for the sanctuary needs yet one that would also address the personal sanctification of the members. Fifty-five women responded to that

1. Herbermann, *Sacristan, Catholic Encyclopedia*.

call and it is one that that is still heard today although that voice may now be a whisper.

The work of an Altar Society assumes a vital role in liturgy. It helps in preparing suitable worship space that assists the congregation in entering into communion with God and each other. While some small parishes and churches do not have official altar societies, they have faithful and trusted women (and no doubt men) who care for the altar in an unobtrusive manner. Some have few members, while other parishes have numerous affiliates such as the St. Francis Altar Society of the Cathedral Basilica of St. Francis of Assisi. Today, the St. Francis Altar Society consists of a group of laywomen who serve their parish located in Santa Fe, New Mexico.

The ministry of the St. Francis Altar Society began in 1921, well before the Second Vatican Council of the 1960s and the call for the laity to be priest, prophet, and king.[2] This book chronicles their mission wherein a few dozen women throughout its history, as the core members, did most of the work. It is a society that has sustained itself for nearly 100 years, truly a formidable accomplishment and a testament to the fortitude of the women as well as the inspiration behind their mission statement. More importantly, the longevity of this group across decades testifies to their devotion to the service of the altar. This shows what that means to them in the Catholic tradition and as a locus wherein they can thrive and find meaning.

In this book, each chapter is devoted to a particular theme that defines the group as co-workers in the vineyard of the Lord [3] partly as a way in which to acknowledge their accomplishments, partly to learn what their history can teach us and other lay ministries. Perhaps most importantly it is to illustrate the meaning of humble service that can be applied in any ministry or personal devotion.

The scope of the history of the St. Francis Altar Society is explored from their deep relationship with flowers as symbolic of their work, to their especial devotion to the Blessed Sacrament, their central ministry of prayer for those who are ill, and their service to "the altar of the world" through acts of mercy and charity for the marginalized both at home and abroad. Their history illustrates their struggles as an organization with membership, their empathy and compassion for others in illness, their persistence with changes in parish rectors, and their responses through world wars and times of change within the church itself.

2. Paul VI, *Dogmatic Constitution.*

3. USCCB, *Co-Workers.*

Through the personal narratives of the 100-year lineage of Presidents and that of other members, a lens is offered of how to view new problems in creative ways and how to sustain and reinterpret their mission so that the altar, parish, and church are served along with the cultivation of the spiritual development of its members. Essentially their biggest challenge has been to balance fidelity to their mission with simultaneously becoming flexible enough to adapt to changing times as many organizations and businesses must also learn to do if they are to survive. As such, for 10 decades, they have succeeded in maintaining their devotion to the altar by reinventing themselves, a skill that is needed in the modern world characterized by rapid change, cultural distractions, and changes in the church. In addition to their history, in this work, forms and templates are provided to those who might wish to form, organize, or improve on an existing altar society.

In today's busy world, with a population of women that are older and have the concomitant obstacles of age, illness, transportation, and even limited income, and a younger audience that have competing activities, the response to that call is not without its problems. As a parish ministerial leader and the most longstanding President, I see that the needs of the Altar Society in many ways parallel the needs of other parish ministries as voluntary organizations that vie for attention and participation in lay ministry.

While the work of the women and the accomplishments of the society over time are told in an anecdotal fashion through interviews, vignettes, written minutes of meetings and meditations, the infrastructure of this work is about the spiritual lineages within the church that animates the society. The Altar Society emerges as an institution where religious, cultural, and social needs are met. Here faithful service is done in small, loving, humble and unobtrusive ways. Since its inception the society has served the literal altar of the church and extended its vision to what I have termed "the altar of the world," through works of world responsibility and social justice which are more urgent than ever, along with the care of the altar and the linens!

Such a society can offer authentic and seasoned spirituality to any age and to those who are older to serve in ministry. Altar Societies fill a role that is indispensible to liturgy and parish life. While some say they are dying breed, I know that altar societies have the opportunity to breathe life into their members and those whom they serve. St. Francis of Assisi continues to capture our imagination and we have emulated his spirit of joyful poverty as we go about our work. There is room in the tradition for the holiness and fidelity of women to serve the church.

Under the mantle of humility, and the commitment to mission, the women of the St. Francis Altar Society have persisted like the women at the foot of the cross. They have embraced the call to ministry and discipleship offered to all in the gospels and one that requires a response. Service to the altar extends beyond the church, into the world, where the reality of the love of Christ intersects with everyday life.

While this is a corporate history book, most of all this is a story of a model of service that illumines what faith in action means. This is the story of the St. Francis Altar Society of the Cathedral Basilica of St. Francis of Assisi and their 100 years of faith in the desert celebrated in 2021! It is very much a story we are all called to live, the call to the altar, and the call to the service of the house of Lord where we all dwell.

SKYA ABBATE
Author and President, 2005–2018

Figure 1 St. Francis Feast Day

1

History

Living Stones of Faith

SOMOS PIEDRAS VIVAS. WE ARE LIVING STONES.

INTRODUCTION

THE UNIQUE HISTORY OF the St. Francis Altar Society is necessarily enmeshed within the geography and community wherein it was founded, grown, and served for almost one hundred years. Here the *Sangre de Cristo Mountains* (Blood of Christ) burn red from the shedding of blood as the sun glows on white mountain snow. In this holy place, from its once dusty, unpaved streets to the pristine polished nave, the Cathedral Basilica of St. Francis of Assisi is a veritable womb where the Roman Catholic faith has both floundered and flourished for over four hundred years. Whether in the stark tranquility of winter or the playful vibrancy of summer, the church and its environs are a peaceful respite in a modern day culture colliding with time. Yet, that peacefulness was gained at the price of conquest, oppression, and finally reconciliation. These deep and extensive roots are important to excavate as the rich historical, social, and spiritual vortex in which the society is embedded.

A Short History

Santa Fe, "The Royal City of Holy Faith of Saint Francis of Assisi, *La Ciudad de Santa Fe de San Francisco de Asis,* sometimes called "the villa" or "the new kingdom of St. Francis," was founded over four hundred years ago in 1610 by Spanish colonists. Spanish Franciscan missionaries who accompanied these explorers then evangelized the inhabitants who had dwelled in this wild land for centuries as Native American tribes. This evangelization by the Franciscans initially took the form of confrontation with the pueblo and semi-nomadic peoples who did not willingly accept baptism. Native resources were plundered along with food, clothing and labor.[1] The newcomers inflicted persecution and pestilence on the proud indigenous cultures that were already replete with their own complex languages, spiritual beliefs, and vibrant traditions. The actions of the Franciscans and Catholic conquerors was an ethos antithetical to the infectious goodness of St. Francis of Assisi, after whom they named the city which silently sits at the foot of the rolling mountains and now the oldest state capital in the United States.

Shortly after the founding of the city in 1625, the small adobe parish church that had been constructed as the precursor to the current Basilica was torn down and a new one was constructed and named the Church of the Assumption. Notably, it housed a pretty, delicately featured three-foot wooden statue of the Blessed Virgin Mary, Our Lady of the Assumption, brought from Spain by Fr. Alonso de Benavides. She was carved from willow wood, most likely in the early 1500s, and holds the infant Jesus in her arms. Her enthronement became the first shrine devoted to the Blessed Mother on the American continent. Soon her name was changed to Our Lady of the Conception, reflecting the popular Church doctrine of the time, specifically that of the Immaculate Conception of Mary. In honor of this invocation of Mary, the Franciscans donned blue habits, not brown as is commonly envisioned.

A significant cultural event in the parish's history that continues to influence its mission, liturgical life, social milieu, and cultural heritage is the Pueblo Indian Revolt of 1680. In that uprising, sparked by the rule of the clerics over the natives,[2] the Native American Indians challenged Spanish rule. Here, they murdered 21 Franciscan priests along with many Indians

1. Nash, *Red, White and Black.*
2. Sanchez, *Nicolas de Aguilar.*

and Spaniards. Subsequently, the persecuted Spaniards fled to Mexico taking with them the statue of the Blessed Virgin Mary, now called Our Lady of the Rosary, also reflecting Church teaching on the power of the rosary as the most trusted weapon in times of danger.[3] This insurrection played a pivotal role in the history of that time and has left behind ruins and racial scars that persist even to this day.

Several years later, in 1693, in the bloodless reconquest of Santa Fe, the Native American Indians were not only defeated but converted to Catholicism, and the statue of Mary was renamed *La Conquistadora,* Our Lady of the Conquest. Spanish leader Don Diego de Vargas, reciting an act of contrition, promised his descendants would forever honor the Virgin Mary if they could return peacefully to their home in Santa Fe. In 1717, the torched church of the 1680 revolt was rebuilt and the remaining *La Conquistadora* Chapel was dedicated to Mary as the intercessor of the peaceful reconciliation and the conversion of 2,000 Native American Indians.

In 1851, the church became the Archbishop's church, that of Archbishop Jean Baptiste Lamy (1875–1885). The cornerstone of the current edifice was laid in 1869, and in 1886 the church was rebuilt in a Romanesque revival style by native residents, carved by Italian stonemasons of local quarried stone, and crowned with a ceiling of volcanic stone and wood from the nearby mountains. Under French ecclesial governance, the church was renamed the Cathedral of St. Francis of Assisi. Architecturally, the church was similar to the Archbishop's native church in France: grandiose and with no hint of its Southwestern nexus except the dry dusty earth upon which it was born. Beautiful stained-glass windows of the four evangelists and the first apostles were installed after their crafting in France. The Cathedral church, although unfinished, was dedicated on March 7, 1886. At that time the church received a simple blessing because the Archbishop knew he would not live for the final completion of the Cathedral. As he expected, shortly thereafter, Archbishop Lamy died in 1888.

The word "Yahweh," the Hebrew name for God, was carved above the main entrance to the Cathedral. Story has it that Archbishop Lamy had it carved to honor his Jewish parents, who contributed to the building of the Cathedral. Although it may have been intended and interpreted as such, the Hebrew inscription is within a triangle, a Christian symbol of the Trinity, which is not part of the Jewish faith. Nevertheless, the carving seems to have both rich personal symbolism for Archbishop Lamy and recognition

3. Hovart, *La Conquistadora.*

of the Jewish roots of Christian faith.[4] Since that time eleven more Archbishops have used the chair in the sanctuary where only Archbishops sit, called Lamy's throne, in their installation ceremonies.

It was not until 9 years later on October 18, 1895, that the church was consecrated, that is, declared sacred and dedicated for religious use. At that point it was complete and debt free due to the generosity of Monsignor Antoine Fourchegu who assumed the entire debt from his inherited wealth. In 1995, according to Archbishop Michael J. Sheehan (1993–2015), "To have a solemn consecration of a Cathedral it has to be completed and paid for." A Cathedral is designated as the center of the liturgical life of a diocese.

In a letter dated September 7, 1895, Archbishop Placid Louis Chapelle (1894–1897) announced that he would receive the *pallium* from Cardinal James Gibbons of Baltimore on October 17, 1895. The *pallium* is a liturgical vestment made of white wool worn over the chasuble symbolizing the bishop as the good shepherd and the Lamb crucified for the human race. It is a symbol of unity with the Pope. Most recently in 2005, when he became the Pope, Benedict XVI proclaimed, "The symbolism of the *pallium* is even more concrete: the lamb's wool is meant to represent the lost, sick or weak sheep which the shepherd places on his shoulders and carries to the waters of life."[5] On October 18, 1895, the third Archbishop of Santa Fe, Placid Louis Chapelle, consecrated the Cathedral during a visit of some distinguished clergy. This included the first cardinal to visit New Mexico, along with a host of priests and witnessed by 3,000 people in attendance.

After a tumultuous history, under the reign of the Republic of Mexico and then as a U.S. Territory, on January 6, 1912, New Mexico joined the Union as the 47th state of the United States. On September 5, 1920 the Franciscan priests from Cincinnati, Ohio assumed charge of the Cathedral on the invitation of Archbishop Albert Thomas Daeger (1919–1932), a Franciscan. One year later, in 1921, the Altar Society was born from the adobe ashes of revolt, reconstruction, and religion, 333 years after the construction of the Church of the Assumption in 1610, the very year Santa Fe was founded. Like the treasured statue of Mary central to the identification of the parish, the Altar Society, called by a recent beloved rector "the backbone of the parish," continues to exist as a vital parish ministry almost 100 years later.

4. Zechmeister and Zechmeister, *The Cathedral Church*, 28.

5. Office of the Liturgical Celebrations, *The Pallium*.

The Franciscans played a fundamental and foundational role in bringing the Catholic faith to the Pueblo Indians but not without the steep price of subjugation and suffering. The first Franciscans arrived with General Juan de Onate from Spain and they staffed the first five churches built on the present site since 1610. After a ninety-four-year absence due to clashes between the friars and bishops, they returned to Santa Fe in the 1920s. In 1995, the Cathedral was the only Cathedral in the United States to be ministered by a religious order: that of the Franciscans.

The chapel of *La Conquistadora,* once part of the original Church of the Assumption, remains as the oldest Marian shrine in the United States. Few know about this treasure, even Catholics, perhaps due to the predominant English view of history. Up to the present day, many miracles have been attributed to her intercession. Reportedly, she was stolen relatively recently in 1973 but found a month later and enshrined in her chapel. Befitting her appellation, Queen of the Kingdom of New Mexico and the Villa of Santa Fe, she is appropriately dressed to coincide with the liturgical seasons from a selection of over three hundred dresses, mantillas, crowns, earrings, and other jewels. This custom of vestimentary overlay followed the tradition of the Spanish. [6] Her original vesture of willow wood, from which she was carved, was adorned in crimson and gold arabesque to resemble a Moorish princess.[7]

La Conquistadora is an integral part of an annual parish novena held every June since that promise to her in exchange for the peace achieved between the Indians and the Spanish under champion Don Diego de Vargas who proclaimed her "the veritable mother who loved them all alike."Likewise, she is the object of great personal and organizational devotion by many parish ministries. *La Conquistadora* was given a new title, Our Lady of Peace, "a 180 degree turn from the longstanding appellation" in 1992 by Archbishop Robert Fortune Sanchez (1974–1993) to reflect the peace ascribed to Mary.[8]

In the 1966 renovation of the Cathedral, a stone casket of two friars who had served the Pueblo Indians was discovered. Both had died in the 1600s. Their remains were transferred to the stone casket in an apse of the parish church located at the Cathedral site in the 1750s. Befittingly, they were later re-interred in the *La Conquistadora* Chapel.

6. McCracken, *La Conquistadora.*
7. Hovart, *La Conquistadora.*
8. McCracken, *La Conquistadora.*

The Cathedral was elevated by Rome to a minor Basilica in 2005. Today its name is the Cathedral Basilica of St. Francis of Assisi. The socio-cultural climate presently is an admixture of the rich cultural blend of Spanish, Caucasian, European, and Native American populaces in a Roman Catholic rite. Those ties are vividly expressed in art, architecture, traditions, mission, liturgy, environmental décor, and even residual tensions. These historical root stories of conflict, conquest, and reconciliation are significant models for the parish's reality as a people of faith. Stemming from this turbulent history, peace is the overarching mission and goal of the parish as it was for its patron, St. Francis of Assisi.

Important Time Lines in the Church History

- 1610 Spanish colonists arrive and the parish church is built
- 1625 The church is named Our Lady of the Assumption
- 1680 The Pueblo Indian Revolt leaves many dead. The Spanish flee to Mexico with Our Lady of the Rosary
- 1693 The Spaniards return to Santa Fe with Our Lady of the Conquest
- 1717 The church is rebuilt
- 1886 The church become a Cathedral
- 1912 New Mexico becomes the 47th the state
- 1921 The St. Francis Altar Society is formed
- 1992 *La Conquistadora* is renamed Our Lady of Peace
- 2005 The church is elevated to a Basilica

The Setting

To further understand the Altar Society an appreciation of Santa Fe itself is necessary. Santa Fe sits at the foot of the *Sangre de Cristo* mountains as part of the southern Rocky mountain chain and holds life in her outstretched palms in a gesture of self-giving. Here eagles and buffalo danced and Spanish horses roamed free in this unique bioregion of high desert terrain. Situated 7,000 feet above sea level, Santa Fe is alternately arrayed by the fruits of the four seasons in a place more bathed in the exuberance of the sun than the coolness of rain. Over 300 days of sunshine penetrate the community of life through howling spring winds, pristine winter snows, golden-hued autumn mountains and green chile summers. Stout native pinon trees, cousins juniper and cedar, adapted to the moistureless air, punctuate the gravelly, sandy soils. Hawks cruise overhead in skies of either interminable blue or crowned with pure white clouds cascading on top of each other in piles like over-stuffed animals. In this quiet terrain only the winds supplant the chatter of birds. Friendly stars, more than you can count, light the dark skies till early morning as the birthday candles of the cosmos that are still having a party almost 15 million years after they were born!

On this natural altar of life, a harmony prevails between animals and plants. The monotone of pinon trees soothes the eyes and marries the earth to the mountains and the sky in a transition from brown to green to blue. Called by the bittersweet fragrances of sunny flowers and the rustle of air in a stream of water the celebration of life starts with the sunrise and ends at its denouement with tumbleweeds blowing across the fields. Mountains bow with snow dripping from their crevices like unclaimed manna. What looks like an economy of scarcity is the promise that what we need will always be there for us.The indigenous modesty of nature is a place to refresh the eyes, to give life to one's breath, a desert Eden that heals and recovers memories that are locked in the earth.

Santa Fe is one of the most spiritual and transformative places in the world. The city's world-renowned arts, opera, religious shrines, blend of ethnic cultures, and cuisine create a vibrant cultural ambiance that counterbalances the tranquility of the surrounding wilderness. Outdoor ventures sit at the city's gate for an active sports life or unobtrusive contemplation. Santa Fe's unique natural beauty makes it a compelling destination for artists, teachers, healthcare practitioners, students, and people searching for a certain quality of life or even transcendental meaning. The local population born from native seeds, hungry migrations, or transplanted by eastern winds cherishes the arid beauty, diverse cultures, and historical mosaic of Santa Fe. Yet, like most cities, Santa Fe has the rich, the poor, and a struggling middle class that tempers its expression.

The parish and the city are not insulated from the economic plight of its inhabitants. While fertile in wild beauty, New Mexico is the poorest state in the United States. The parish and city are sensitized to the poverty and injustices in its midst. The city, church, and state strive to reach out as the veritable heart of Santa Fe in their lifeblood of service to the impoverished.

Its Hispanic roots, the Catholic nature of the city, and Catholic social doctrine predispose the parish to empathic service. Santa Fe has concerns for social justice issues such as poverty, homelessness, childhood health and hunger, and the conditions that accompany those situations.

Santa Fe is one of 130–200 sanctuary cities in the United States that offer protection and assistance to illegal immigrants. Ministries within the parish such as the St. Vincent de Paul Society, the Liturgy Committee, and the St. Francis Altar Society also feed the hungry, provide clothing, alms, and other services on an on-going basis to the needy.

Today the city is still small, with only approximately 143,000 people. This size perhaps is one of the secrets to the preservation of its spectacular natural beauty, historic sites, and cultural traditions. The lack of heavy industry also safeguards this powerful geographic area. Santa Fe's primary industry is tourism and the popularity of Santa Fe as a tourist destination contributes to its cultural preservation. The Basilica is a focal point for downtown tourist attractions as one of the most beautiful churches in the United States.

The physical environment and liturgical celebrations of a Basilica have Roman Catholic requirements to reflect its heritage, in this case its Caucasian, Hispanic, and Latin (Roman) influences. The parish partially achieves this diversity through language in song and chants in English, Spanish, and Latin respectively. That heritage is augmented in the decoration of the church in art forms such as religious European oil paintings, devotions to Mary, Hispanic altar screens, cloths and art, and its Stations of the Cross rendered in a native, two-dimensional art form. Throughout its history, the members of the Altar Society have promoted and maintained these traditions through their monetary donations to the parish for the maintenance and beautification of the church, such as the purchase of pews, pianos, and furniture as well as through their weekly cleaning of the church and their participation in the parish's rich liturgical celebrations.

Today, the Cathedral Basilica of St. Francis of Assisi, as perhaps the most recognizable symbol of Santa Fe, rivals the greatest world churches as a place of divine inspiration. The holy faith of St. Francis of Assisi (1181–1226) is emblazoned in the parishioners of the Basilica and in particular in the hearts of the St. Francis Altar Society members, true living stones of faith constructed in response to the call of service to the altar of the church and the world. Akin to *La Conquistadora*, the Altar Society is an enduring, longstanding, and living icon of the parish. Hopefully like she who can conquer human hearts through faith and establish peace, and the saint after which it is named, the society will continue do the same through its spirit of simple joy and giving.

As the coyotes serenade the last of the night, a half-moon shines its guiding rays till the morn. The silver sage absorbs its light. Life is sustained and amplified by a secret heart that is compelled to hold the high desert sacred in wild, stirring repose. It is the edge of the world where humans meet the heart of God. You can call it the wild or creation. You can call it Santa Fe or the city of holy faith. But you must at least be sure to call it by its rightful name. You must call it love.

The Santa Fe Trail Days, August 1977 Reflection

By Mrs. Lyle Quintana Johnson, Altar Society President, 1975–1977

With the Treaty of Guadalupe Hidalgo, the United States Government officially took over New Mexico in 1848 from the Republic of Mexico soon bringing different customs, different language, and even different religious practices for the populace to cope with. With the change of social conditions, the native people gradually were drawn out of their self-sufficient ways and New Mexican religious folk art became something of the past; a way of life gone forever.

One of Archbishop Lamy's reforms after he arrived in his newly created diocese in 1851 was an order to discard the *Santos.* * To his European eyes, they were grotesque. He directed that they be replaced with conventional plaster images and colored lithographs from France. Further, in 1854, a company of French priests was sent to the diocese upon the request of Archbishop Lamy. It was only natural that these new fathers, too, found little appeal in the simple folk art of a people who were of another cultural background. Nothing was done to encourage local artistic tradition, as evidenced by the erection of the Santa Fe Cathedral in a style completely divorced from its surroundings. Most of the *Santos* were destroyed but not all; a few lingered in lonely chapels and rural homes. It was necessary for more than half a century to elapse before these neglected *Santos* became objects of interest and appeal.

*A *Santos* is a wooden statue carved in a New Mexican folk art style.

President Skya Abbate, 2012 Historical Reflection

A New Englander's Transplant to the Southwest and the Nature of Conquest

While it is possible that Europeans came to our continent to learn what it had to teach us about the divine, how we might live, and how we might relate to other life forms, the fact of the matter is that this is not why our ancestors travelled to the North American continent. It would seem that there is some truth that we cannot find what we are not looking for. And so their paradigmatic outlook blinded them from the inexpressible beauty and wildness. Their vision was blocked by their heavy metal helmets and stiff hats to a world more suited to the lightness of feathers woven in the hair of the indigenous peoples that could catch the breeze as a whisper from a nearby God.

As we contemplate our shared American history, essentially culture is about what we share. Our first ancestors, the Spanish, came to America, a place envisioned as dripping with gold; gold to make Catholic kings, and queens, and adventurers rich. Instead, they met the Native American Indians of the Southwest, those with burnished skin, living in golden fields and riding golden mustangs, people who did not know Jesus Christ, but who saw the self-expression of God in nature that defined the borders of their lives. The Pilgrims who arrived later to the New England shore came to seek freedom from religious persecution in Europe, not to find a new face of God in the Indian tribes that they soon displaced. They had a concept of him as more righteous than loving, and when one lives in a world conditioned by sin and fear, even moving to a new shore will not change that world of immovable hearts.

It is hard to escape culture—it is so pervasive—it shapes us from the womb to the grave.So it is unfair to pass judgment on them and what they forfeited as they clung to the security of what they knew. The gift they gave us was leaving their homelands for whatever reason to go and live in a new place that is now our home. It is notably ironic that those who believed in Jesus Christ, as English Protestants, Catholic Spaniards, French, Portuguese, and Germans of mixed faith, did not understand the Jesus of love. Jesus is not the exclusion, or death of the Indians and animals they encountered, or the rape of the land they saw ripe for the taking.

What was to become New England had the wild waves of the Atlantic Ocean, frigid winters, and ferocious animals. The Southwest had its simmering heat, stifling dryness, and massive buffalo and these were new realities that could have evoked a transformation of being. In essence, the explorers and immigrants lacked the liturgical imagination to see God in their brown-skinned brothers and sisters and in the wonder of a Southwest sunset or a New England "Indian" summer. They carried images with them from the old world of what life was and sought to recreate it in a foreign land.

Things could have been so different if the canvas of America had been painted with bold native pigments with which to capture the world, if they could have beheld the pristine beauty of the curious expressions of flora and fauna that they were not used to. That life was the manifestation of nature's cleverness if not the actual workings of a world longing to express itself, or a God of wisdom, power, and awe, not a strict and punishing one. America could have been the new world of possibility in harmony, instead a world of conquest. Life, the lessons learned, and the alternative dream of a true arcadia could have been realized. Future generations, learning from the lessons of a history of violence against the Native Americans, a people living so intimately in nature as a living membrane of life and an inextricable web to which they were happily connected, could have taught our ancestors lessons of how to live peacefully, in interdependence, reverence, wonder of the deer, the corn, the stars and the very face of God.

Perhaps the grandeur of the landscape and the soaring of the eagle did on some level shape their consciousness so that they could dream of a place, defined by law, that was a place of freedom. It would take them many years to learn how to interpret that freedom and apply it to people of color, women, children, animals and the earth. This is our true heritage.

Retrospectively we can see their faux pas. The dream of the Indian and the dream of the white man are not incompatible but they are not yet completed. Together they can create a world of biospirituality, if we, their descendants will but listen to the distant drums that signal the dream that the earth is dreaming in its unfolding.

Figure 2 The Cathedral Basilica of St. Francis of Assisi

PRAYER OF THE ST. FRANCIS ALTAR SOCIETY

Oh God of infinite graces, you invite us to your holy altar.

We are allowed into your limitless life to care and provide for your church.

Our humble hands and fervent hearts are made whole and happy in your presence.

The linens of our making and the flowers of your creation are tokens of our love for you.

We adore you in the Most Blessed Sacrament, and in the tabernacle of our heart.

Bless us your servants when we are in your house, and with St. Francis of Assisi our patron,

May all we do be a quiet, thoughtful, thankful and joyful witness

Of your enduring love, sacrifice and mercy.

With Jesus as our future and Mary as our guide

We will do all that you ask in the brightness of our household of faith

As we make our way with the Lamb to our eternal home+ Amen

Skya Abbate, President, 2005–2018

2

Mission and Institutional Realities

"The Work of the Altar Should be a Labor of Love"

MISSION OF THE ST. FRANCIS ALTAR SOCIETY

> The primary purpose of the society shall be the care of the altars and sanctuary and their needs; to make our total church environment hospitable and fit for worship; to promote the personal sanctification of the members through participation in special liturgical celebrations and processions, and to observe First Friday Adoration of the Blessed Sacrament. The secondary purpose is to promote sociability among our parish community by lending assistance with pastoral projects and social events. (Mission Statement, 2017)

THE BEGINNING

Little did he know (or perhaps he did), that when he summoned the women of the parish to care for the altar and sanctuary, that on February 10, 1921, much akin to the summons to St. Francis of Assisi to rebuild his (Jesus') church, that 55 women in the parish of St. Francis of Assisi in Santa Fe, New Mexico would respond to that call! Almost one hundred years later that invitation by Fr. Eligius Kunkel is still heard today by the women of the

St. Francis Altar Society, although the call now may mimic a whisper. The contemporary challenge posed to the members is to make that invitation heard more loudly today and responded to in the future.

As charter members, this first group of women selected the colors of St. Francis at that time, the humble colors of brown and white to symbolize the organization. They adopted the motto, "The work of the altar should be a labor of love," a maxim that has continued to direct the work of the society to the present time. To do that work the women decided to meet on the third Monday of every month and this stayed true until the year 2000, when it changed to the third Wednesday of the month to accommodate the schedule of the Spiritual Director whom they were very fond of. This long-term commitment was certainly a testimony to the fidelity of the women to the service of the altar.

Originally, only women were able to be Altar Society members and this was true for most of the society's history until language was changed in the Constitution to open it to all. Thereafter, both exemplary men and problematic ones joined the society briefly. Overall, it has been thought of as a "woman's organization,"[1] as most parish altar societies have historically been viewed.

Under the guidance of the first President, Mrs. May Murphy, in 1921, the initial Constitution and By-Laws were drawn up. The primary purposes as interpreted by the society were twofold. Firstly, it was dedicated to the personal sanctification of the members and secondarily to the care for the altar and sanctuary and their needs, to work for the church in general, and to promote sociability amongst Catholic women. It is interesting to see that around 1957, the twofold purposes were reprioritized and reversed.

The leadership positions created were President, Vice President, Financial Secretary, Recording Secretary, Treasurer and Spiritual Director. The terms of office were to last for one calendar year beginning in January. Standing Committees that organized the work of the society included but were not limited to Spiritual Formation, Altar and Sanctuary, Ways and Means, Organizational Development, Family Education, Community Action and World Responsibility.

Throughout their history the women responded with concern not only to the literal altar of the church, but to the broader interpretation of what I have termed "the altar of the world" through their charity and service to the parish, city, state, nation and world. As documented through their minutes

1. Dolan, *Transforming*, 2.

and articles in the local newspapers and awards they received, that charity has continued to distinguish the society throughout its long history.

Over the years the Constitution and By-Laws were revised and amended fourteen times. What can be discerned as significant changes are detailed herein.

Constitutional Changes

- 1921

  The original Constitution was chartered

- 1947

  Only women could be members

  Personal sanctification of the women was the primary purpose

  Elections were held annually and by majority vote

  The meetings were held on the 3rd Monday of the month at 3 p.m.

  The society was a Member of the National Council of Catholic Women and the Santa Fe Archdiocesan Council of Catholic Women

  The Constitution and the By-Laws may be amended at any regular meeting by majority vote

  Any member failing to pay dues for a year shall be considered delinquent and not entitled to any privileges or benefits of the society

  The President may at any time call a special meeting at which time no business can be transacted except that which is specified in the call

  The Altar and Sanctuary Committee shall have the charge of the Altar and Sanctuary

  The Sewing Committee shall be responsible for the mending of altar linens and vestments

  The Membership Committee shall endeavor to increase the membership of the society by contacting Catholic women of the parish

The Ways and Means Committee shall have the responsibility of raising funds for the society when necessary

The President shall appoint a Nominating Committee in November, consisting of three members, who shall prepare a ticket containing the names of the candidates for the offices, to be elected at the annual meeting in January

A monthly low Mass was to be said for all living and deceased members

- 1957

  A By-Laws Committee was established which seemed to be related to Corporate Communion

  The monthy meeting will be held Monday evening at the Catholic Maternity Institute

- 1965, 1972 not known
- 1974

  The twice-yearly evening meetings were changed to daytime

- 1977

  Membership dues increased from $6.00 to $10.00

  The Constitution may be amended only by a two-thirds vote of those present at the meeting, provided that the proposed amendment has been read at two previous meetings

- 1984

  Masses were paid for by the donation of cash contributions for sick members and their families

- 1988

  The 1984 amendment was nullified. Money for Masses for sick members was now to come from the general fund

- 1994, not known
- 2000

Monthly meetings changed from the third Monday to third Wednesday of every month at 1:30 pm to accommodate the schedule of the Spiritual Director

A rosary will be said for a deceased immediate member "when the member or family requests it"

- 2009

  The Constitution and By-Laws of this society may be amended, altered, repealed and new ones adopted by a 51 percent vote of those members present at any regular or special meeting, provided that the proposed amendment has been read at one previous regular meeting

- 2017

  Society name changed from the St. Francis Altar Society to the St. Francis Altar Society of the Cathedral Basilica of St. Francis of Assisi

  Society colors changed to brown, white, and green

  Adoration of Blessed Sacrament—deleted"whenever possible" to strengthen the idea of adoration and to read " to observe First Friday Adoration of the Blessed Sacrament"

  Membership dues increase from $15.00 to $25.00

An existing booklet in Spanish dated 1940, and referenced in the minutes, shows that apparently there was a separate Spanish Altar Society at the Cathedral. Both societies merged in 1949 to consolidate national dues. The Spanish By-Laws are very interesting, especially as pertains to the death of members and the women's role in honoring that loss. A careful translation of that book, *Reglamento*, follows.

Regulations of the Altar Society

Article 1.

The Altar Society established in this Cathedral, has finally created a fund, exclusively for the purchase of the objects necessary for a decent and complete service to the Altar.

Article 2.

This Society is formed as follows: There shall be a priest in charge of it, who shall be the Director, President and Treasurer of the same; and its members shall be the (married) ladies and the young ladies of the Catholic families of this Cathedral parish.

Article 3.

The Director shall select an adequate number of Society members, and shall put each one of them in charge of a neighborhood (or area) of this parish; said Society members shall have the name of Collectors.

Article 4.

Each Society member of the Altar shall contribute the membership fee of 15 cents a month for the purpose of the Society; each Collector shall collect the membership fee from the Society members who live in the neighborhood of which she is in charge.

Article 5.

The admission of the members shall be done in the following way: The person who wishes to be admitted shall inform the Collector of her neighborhood; she (the Collector) present the request in a special meeting, to the other Collectors and the Director; who shall decide in common agreement to admit or reject the said person (candidate).

Article 6.

Whenever there is a death or separation of one of the Collectors, it requires the promotion of another member to take her place, the Director and the Collectors, in a Special Meeting, shall name the person, who in their judgment is competent for that charge.

Article 7.

A Mass shall be celebrated for all the members of the Altar Society, each month on a day that shall be conveniently set; and they shall hold a meeting on the second Sunday. In this meeting the Rosary of 5 Mysteries shall be recited with the Litanies of the Blessed Virgin Mary; special prayers for the Society, enriched by the Most Reverend Archbishop, with 40 days indulgences applicable for the faithful departed; and the observances most conducive for the greatest success of the Society shall be done. The Collectors, especially, must attend these meetings, so they can do their monthly report at the end of the meetings.

Article 8.

When one of the Altar Society members dies, the Collector of her neighborhood shall inform the Director and shall take the Altar Society banner to the house of the deceased, to place it before the body; afterwards she shall notify the other Society members that belong to the neighborhood of the deceased, concerning the death and the day of the funeral of the said deceased Society member.

Article 9.

All the Society members that are able, and especially those that belong to the neighborhood of the deceased, shall meet at the home of the deceased on the day of her funeral, so they can lead the body, preceded by the Director, to the Cathedral and then to the Cemetery.

Article 10.

The Collectors, being attentive to their services (duties), in addition to directing the funeral in the manner previously described, shall see that each Society member in general, carries out their responsibility, and shall have a Mass offered on the eighth day with two tolls of the bell; offering a stipend of $3.00 for the Mass to be taken.

Article 11.

The prayers for the dead that this Society shall offer for each of its members shall be: To offer a Mass with all the Society members together, a Communion, and a Rosary of 5 Mysteries, within the first month of the death of the Society member, on the day that shall be conveniently set.

Article 12.

Any Society member, that fails to pay the membership fee for three continuous months, without a justified reason, shall no longer be able to belong to the Altar Society.

The Social Context of the Altar Society

The Cathedral Basilica of St. Francis of Assisi is geographically located in the heart of Santa Fe, New Mexico, in the small downtown area one block east of the central plaza. Today it is a minor Basilica and a Cathedral, which is considered the Archbishop's church. Under this structure, the Archbishop is designated as the pastor and the rector is the presiding priest who oversees the parish.

The contemporary socio-cultural climate of the parish is a vibrant faith community of predominantly 1,486 registered households composed of approximately 2,665 individuals, a parish that continues to grow from deep Franciscan and Spanish roots. The parish is made up of a preponderance of Hispanic and Caucasian people with some Native American ancestry. A mosaic of African Americans and other racial and ethnic groups rounds out its complexion.

Santa Fe is the capital of an economically poor state, the poorest state in the nation, but a state steeped in religious tradition. The parish, through its active members and long, historical past, acts as an important mediating structure for the members. It affords opportunities for faith enrichment through travel, social events, participation in liturgy, and over 30 ministries that support the whole person and the needs of the parish and the community. The parish and the Altar Society extend themselves beyond church walls through their charitable outreach such as caring for the homeless through the provision of seasonal meals at an interfaith shelter, monthly donations to nondenominational groups that need financial assistance, and care of the poor and hungry through monthly and yearly food drives for the local St. Vincent de Paul store, to name a few of these activities.

Demographics of the Members

As Santa Feans, the Altar Society honors the age, ethnicity, cultures and members' unique gifts by learning about their history. In March 2017, a questionnaire was mailed to the 63 members of the society to collect demographics on the membership. A 51 percent return rate, which is considered quite high, was achieved. Still, one might wonder why it was not higher. Some of that information is summarized here and other parts are introduced in later chapters. This data serves as a springboard to the future course of the society that is analyzed within this book.

As of this writing, the constituents are women, 60–95 years old as depicted in figure 3. Most members are married or widowed as seen in figure 4. Virtually all are retired as figure 5 illustrates. Men are not precluded from membership and have been members in the past. Regrettably some situations led to the sexual harassment of the women and the offenders were asked to leave through the intercession of the Spiritual Director. Socio-economically, most of the ladies are of the middle class, and from that relative comfort and work ethic, coupled with age, retirement, or identification with the mission of the Altar Society, they have the time for consistent,

Ages
14
12
10
8
6
4
2
0
40's
50's
60's
70's
80's
95

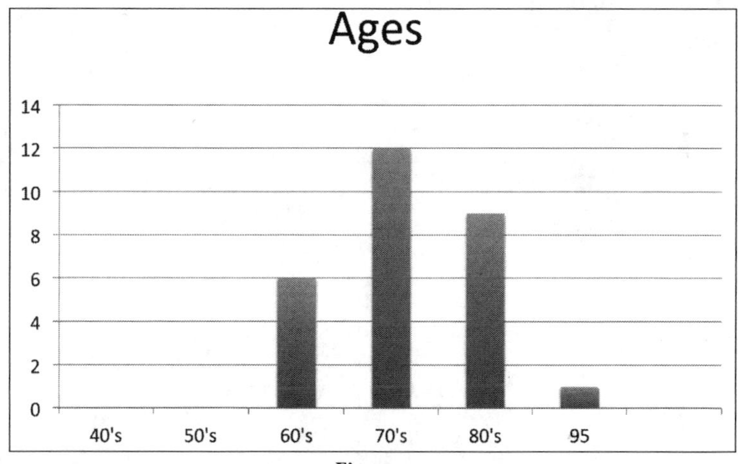

Figure 3

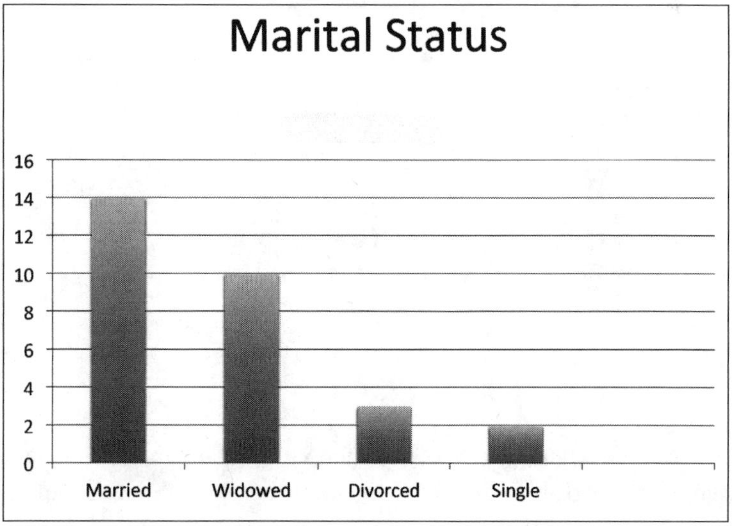

Marital Status
16
14
12
10
8
6
4
2
0
Married
Widowed
Divorced
Single

Figure 4

monthly participation at meetings, weekly cleaning of the church, and washing and ironing of the holy cloths, seasonal decoration of the church, and hostessing various parish and archdiocesan functions.

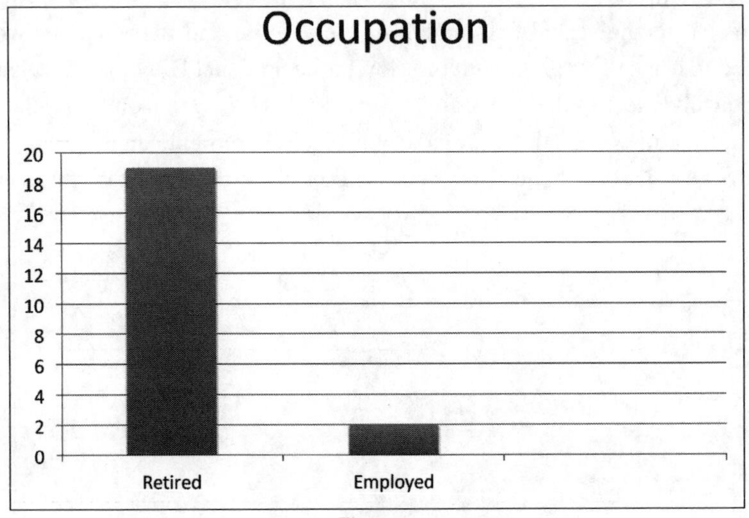

Figure 5

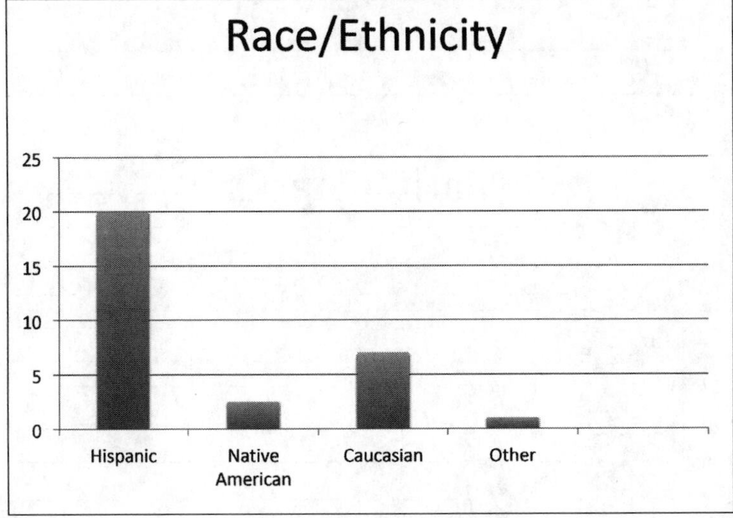

Figure 6

Approximately 60 percent of the women are Hispanic and the balance is Caucasian as seen in figure 6. Their education spans high school to the doctoral level illustrated in figure 7. None have belonged to other Altar

Societies. In the survey, it was revealed that the preponderance of the women has been in the society for 6 to over 20 years thus illustrating their devotion to the organization and the altar seen in figure 8. Membership

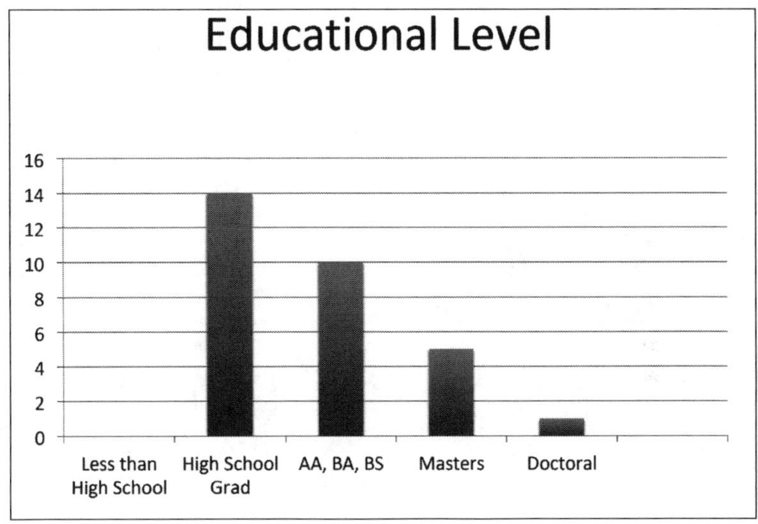

Figure 7

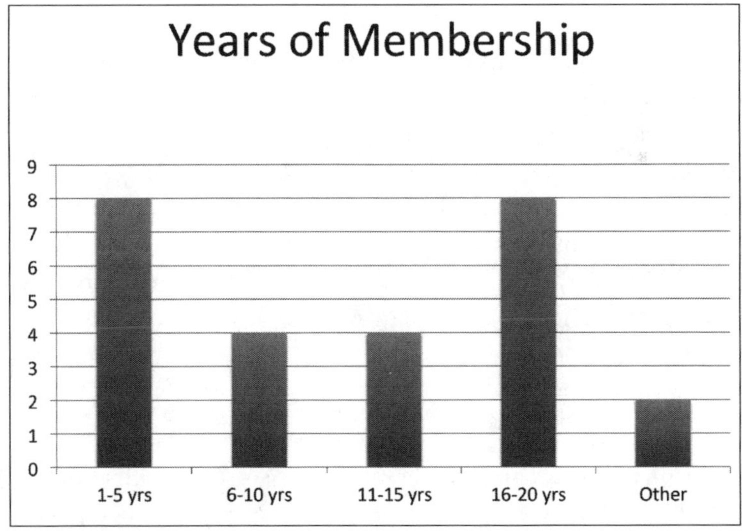

Figure 8

cards, which the society retains, indicate that many have been members for over forty years! The members participate in the society by identifying with its mission and for socializing, along with other tasks the society is involved with such as Blessed Sacrament Adoration, the prayer ministry, and for personal and spiritual development as figure 9 shows.

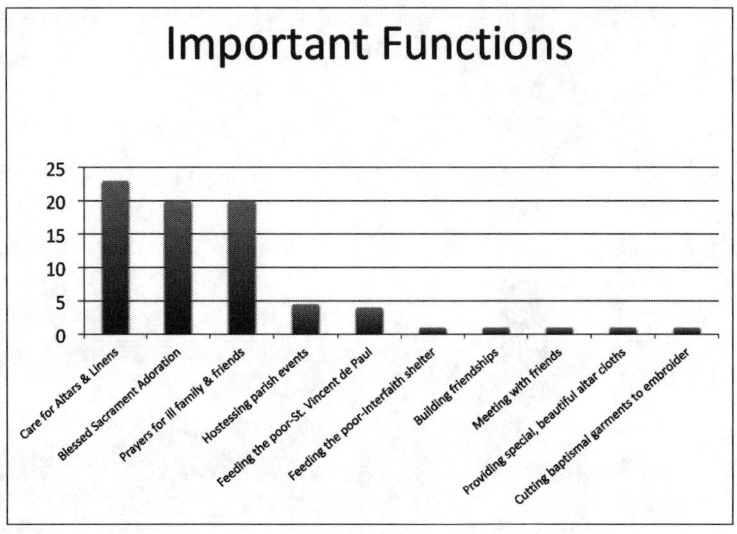

Figure 9

The work of the society has largely been the same over time as directed by its mission statement. Obviously, historical circumstances have affected some activities such as the recipients of charitable donations and the types of committees that organized the society's work. In a very pure way, the women have remained faithful to the original motto of the Altar Society conceived in 1921 by the first ladies who responded to the call of Fr. Eligius and no doubt that of the Holy Spirit! Theirs is a labor of love for the glory of God attested to in their history and ongoing service.

Coming to Understand the Mission

The mission statement of the St. Francis Altar Society, found at the beginning of this chapter, and expressed in its Constitution, accurately encapsulates its purpose, values, and vision. It is a mission that has sustained the society throughout many changes although those changes have not always been easy. The story of these challenges is documented in the minutes and told in the chapters on the Years, the Presidents, and the Personalities.

The society's Catholic outlook vastly deepens and supplements the idea of their ministerial involvement as greater than the literal tasks detailed in the mission statement. The Altar Society does many things under a broad interpretation of its mission statement such as serving food at parish events, which in some churches is performed by a Hospitality Committee; and collecting monthly bags of food for the St. Vincent de Paul store. The society cooks, brings food, and serves it at various parish events. For the preponderance of its history the women greatly enjoyed flower purchasing and liturgical decoration as a core part of their mission but this participation is waning due to organizational changes in the parish. Cleaning the church and being alone with the Lord in the sanctuary, the holiest of holy places in the church, or washing and ironing the linens, continues to be one of the most cherished times and for this alone many are happy to be members.

In the society, no member is required to do any particular task. Some women like cleaning, while others prefer laundry or cooking. Some like attending meetings, others making phone calls. As new members become acclimated to the society they tend to choose the jobs that they like and overall this works out well. Regardless of the task the members are called to do, the society is invited to interpret its ministry as discipleship. This discipleship is tested especially in the things that might be disliked!

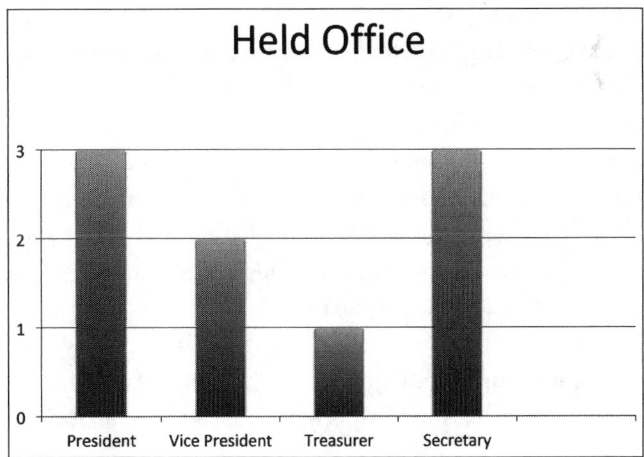

Figure 10

Lately, it has been increasingly difficult getting members to assume leadership positions. For instance, the current President has held this position for 14 years when the norm has been 1–2 years! The Treasurer has been in this position for 18 years. These allowances have been secured through exemption of the By-Laws. Secretaries tend to serve their two-year elected term. Vice Presidents have been hard to solicit even though that office requires essentially making phone calls. This is an area that the society must grapple with to create hybrid vigor, stimulate service, and ensure the society's survival. Figure 10 shows how many have held office.

Like the first Christians who understood Pentecost as "a democratizing experience" where "the gifts of the Spirit were to be used by all for the good of all,"[2] that is, every person mattered for who they were and who they were relationally to the community, the same is true for the Altar Society. Practically augmented by St. Paul's concept of charisms as individual God-giftedness for the sake of community, the society strives to recognize and reinforce these gifts by encouraging the members to offer their talents in ever-widening circles of service, compassion, and transformation within the society, the parish, and the world.

The group's initial understanding of its ministry is connected with three integrated points—the utilization of personal gifts, in service to others, and in a manner that can afford a way to morally live in the world. What sustains membership is the mission of the care of the altar, Adoration of the Blessed Sacrament, desire for a social connection with the parish in ministry, especially liturgy, cultivation of church environment, and pastoral leadership. The current President sees the society's comprehension of its ministry as evolving in that is not as much about what it does as about how it is done, that is, ideally through love.

The challenge for the members is to create opportunities to ameliorate any organizational weaknesses by increasing organizational understandings and effective executive leadership. In sharing, the members can grow in personal sanctification and obtain a deeper understanding of the church and the world. Even the most trivial administrative tasks become an occasion for a divine-human encounter.[3] Work is not merely something the members perform, for a Catholic theology of work cannot be antithetical to a theology of service. The work is a manifestation of a labor of love for the glory of God.

Tradition offers insight into the praxis of the society. St. Francis of Assisi is the patron saint of the parish and the Altar Society. According to

2. Bernier, *Ministry*, 20.

3. Brunner in Brown, *Seward*, 115.

the story, in the dilapidated church at San Damiano, Italy, Francis heard Jesus say, "Rebuild my church." Francis literally interpreted this to mean to fix up the building, and so he did. Later, he realized that the church Jesus was referring to was the spirit of the church. Francis then devoted his life to this idea.

Like Francis, the group works to beautify the physical church. But going a step further it aims at establishing peace amongst the members of the society and the parish as an authentic meaning of church. Through action the members work to demonstrate the faith, peace, and charity Francis emulated. Through a deep love of nature, Mary, and the joy of holy poverty, the members use his life as a model by which to live. They treasure Francis' mystical, yet natural union with creation, especially flowers, as a society that bears his name. The group values the "peace" of Mary Our Lady of Peace, and that of Francis and seeks to maintain it in all its interactions.

Retreat 2016

3

Organization

Oasis of Grace in the Desert

"Draw me: We will run."

Song of Solomon 1:3

ORGANIZATION

In order to accomplish the overall mission of the society—the care of the altar, the sanctuary, and sacristies—and the coordination of the liturgical seasons with the work of the society, the St. Francis Altar Society meets nine times a year in the afternoon, on the third Wednesday of every month with the exception June, July, and December. The first meetings were held mostly on Mondays and in 2000 moved to Wednesdays. July is slow liturgically and so the group pauses for an annual retreat to refresh and renew personal relationships, cultivate group spirituality, and rededicate themselves to the society's mission. In December there is much decoration to be done so those members who are available help decorate the Basilica for Christmas with the arrangement of poinsettias, Christmas trees, wreaths, and other decorations. The decoration and the celebration of the new liturgical year with the birth of our Savior supplant the meeting.

Monthly, the group assembles in one of the small parish meeting rooms on the church property. The downtown venue is convenient for assembling. For most of the group's history it met in members' homes, at the Santa Fe Maternity Hospital, and in a hotel until the parish meeting room became available in 1980.

The monthly meetings generally last an hour and a half, from 1:30–3:00 p.m. The meetings begin with welcomes in words and embraces, a call to order, and recitation of the *Altar Society Prayer* recently written in 2012 by President Skya Abbate and adopted by the membership. Since its inception the Altar Society has followed a standardized format in the conduct of its meetings through Parliamentary Procedure to ensure order, decision-making, and action.

After the opening prayer, an informal Spiritual Director's report traditionally preceded the business. Next, the Secretary reads the previous month's minutes followed by any corrections or amendments. Up until 2005, the minutes were fleshed out on typewriters, yet there were a few years when the minutes were carefully handwritten in clean penmanship on onionskin paper! In 2005 the computer became the new mechanism for transcribing the minutes.

Following the minutes is the reading of correspondence that the society frequently receives from those for whom we have Masses said such as for those who are ill, or for family members of those who have died, and from those to whom we send gifts to such as clergy for birthdays, Christmas, anniversary remembrances, or going away gifts. We then report on friends, family, or members who may need prayers. The Treasurer arranges for a Mass to be said for members at the nearby Carmelite monastery. Immediately following these remembrances, we say an "*Our Father*" for the deceased and ill, for our own intentions, and in thanksgiving for our blessings. This prayer for the ill serves as a central part of the society's identification, which unites us spiritually as a group and with the Communion of Saints. The members rightly recognize that this prayer is ministry. Next, the Treasurer reports on the finances of the year to date through a monthly report.

Sign-ups sheets are circulated for the monthly cleaning of the church, the washing and ironing of the holy cloths, for provision of flowers in the Blessed Sacrament Chapel for First Friday Adoration, and for monthly hostesses. With the exception of Advent and Lent, when flowers are not permitted in the church, two or three members purchase seasonal flowers for First Friday Adoration with their own money in honor of the Blessed Sacrament, which is an especial devotion of the society. The Altar Society representative to the Pastoral Council delivers a report to the group on their news. Then a Liturgy Committee Report by the Liturgy Committee Representative, who is the President, is made. The interface of the Liturgy Committee with the Altar Society ensures the coordination of the work of the liturgical year such as decorating or hostessing receptions following Masses. The names and numbers of the committees have changed over time reflecting the needs of the group within their historical matrix. Old Business, New Business, announcements, closing prayer and adjournment follow. A sample agenda that structures the meeting can be found in chapter 12.

At this time the Altar Society has fewer committees than it had in the past. Today they include the Altar and Sanctuary Committee and representatives to the Liturgy Committee and the Pastoral Council. Each of the approximately 30 ministries participates in the Pastoral Council. The newly reinstituted Membership Committee and Flower Committee are starting to report.

The heart of the Altar Society is the Altar and Sanctuary Committee. The women in this committee maintain the weekly cleaning of the church and the washing and ironing of the holy clothes used during Mass. These linens include the lavabos (the terry-cloth towels used by the priest to wash his hands in preparation for the consecration), the priest and Eucharistic minister purificators (the linen hand towels that come in contact with the precious blood administered during Communion), and the corporals (the linen that is placed on the altar and upon which the chalice and ciboria rest during the consecration that symbolizes the shroud that Jesus was laid in). All of these linens, with the exception of the lavabos (that do not touch the host or precious blood), require special laundering due to their contact with the consecrated species of bread and wine. Also, with the exception of the lavabos, all of the linens must be washed and ironed in a particular way. The detailed care of the holy cloths can be found in chapter 12.

Luckily, some members prefer to care for the linens, others to clean the church. Weekly, two members clean the church every Friday on a monthly rotation basis. The cleaning is light work but the Basilica is large. It takes about two hours to change the holy water in the finger bowls and dust the sacristies, sanctuary, confessionals, and the nave and its furniture. The members also clean the small Blessed Sacrament Chapel (also called

St. Joseph's Chapel) within the Basilica where daily Mass is said and Adoration held. Up until last year the Altar Society cleaners replaced the votive candles, supplemented by the sacristan throughout the week, due to the high volume of tourists at the Basilica who offer their intentions through the light of a candle. Now due to a new candle system, the sacristan alone replenishes the candles.

A historical review of the Altar Society illustrates the many other committees they had to structure the work of the mission. The committees for much of the Altar Society history were membership, Ways and Means, Publicity, World Responsibility, Community Action, Spiritual Development, Friendly Visitors, and Charity. Today much of this work continues but is subsumed within the overall work of the society. For instance, there are mechanisms within the group for spiritual development such as the annual retreat, the monthly prayers for friends and families, Adoration of the Blessed Sacrament, and the writing of this book. However, in consideration of the number of current members and their ages, declining participation in the society, and the decreased willingness or ability of the members in assuming leadership positions and decorating and hostessing, the reinstitution of the Membership Committee combined with a Publicity Committee could assist in recruiting new members. With more committees the work could be distributed more equitably and leadership promoted. The work the members do in the society is illustrated in figure 12.

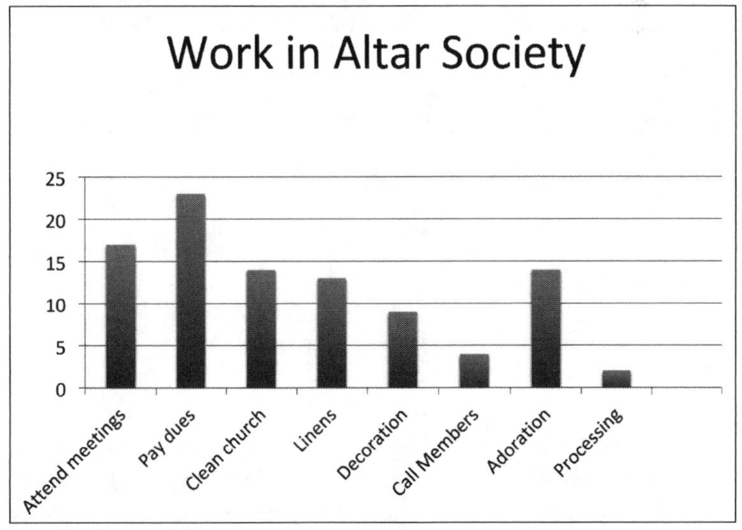

Figure 12

Many members also belong to other parish ministries as seen in figure 13. On occasion those ministries may conflict with Altar Society meetings and events, thus vying for the members' time. Approximately half of the members do not come to the meetings. They pay dues and may actively participate by making phone calls but just not attend the meetings. While the 2017 survey had a 51 percent response rate, which is considered high, yet still 30 members did not respond even when a free stamp was provided to return the questionnaire. It is hard to interpret the significance of the lack of response but it parallels the lack of participation other than paying membership dues. This is a common American phenomenon in voluntary organizations, that is, members are willing to pay dues but many may be less involved in an organization that they have freely joined due to competing activities or desire to be more active. In the case of the Altar Society the impact of age, illness, incapacity or problems with transportation that the women experience cannot be forgotten.

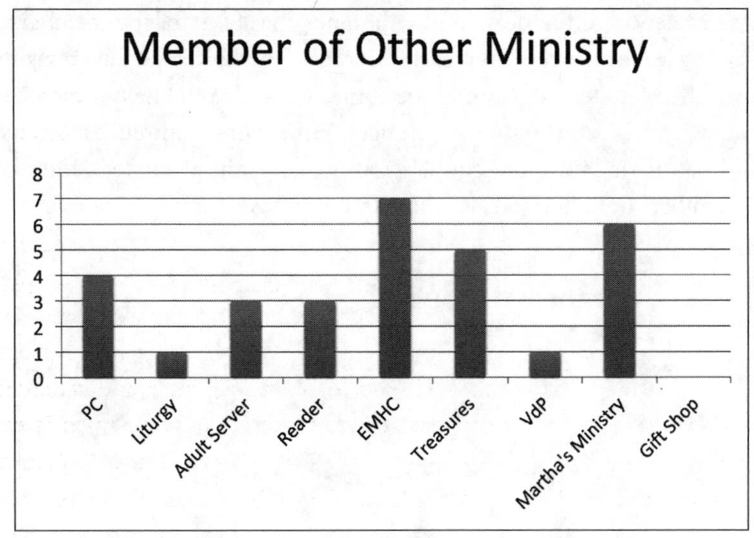

Figure 13

Officers

Today there are six officers of the St. Francis Altar Society, that of President, Vice President, Treasurer, Secretary, Past President and Spiritual Director. The formal job description of President specifies the role of serving as the chair at meetings and appointing all standing committees. The President composes the agendas, heads up social events, assists in planning and running the annual retreat, promotes Adoration of the Most Blessed Sacrament, and serves as the representative to the Liturgy Committee. Many other activities fall within the role of President and need to be interpreted with a wide-angled lens. In short, the President often does what needs to be done.

The Vice President calls the food hostesses every month to remind them to prepare the light lunch following the meeting. The Vice President also calls the Telephone Captains who in turn call the members on their list about meetings and special events. The Secretary takes the minutes and prepares them for the subsequent monthly meeting to be read, amended, and adopted. The Treasurer reports on income and expenditures and maintains the financial accounts. The Past President trains the new President. The Spiritual Director is the rector of the parish and approves of all new members.

Money is generated from the annual membership dues, recently changed in 2018 from $15 to $25 and that cumulatively amounts to about $1,500 a year. This income makes up the operating budget for yearly expenses that are not related to the needs of the sanctuary. From membership money the society pays for Masses for ill and deceased friends and families, and gives gifts to clergy, religious, and maintenance workers. The society donates to international and local charities and participates in parish projects, such as buying commemorative bricks for the prayer garden and other church furnishings. The Altar Society assists the youth on their trips to World Youth Day and annually meets, greets, prays with, and feeds the *peregrinos* (pilgrims) who walk for vocations throughout New Mexico.

An annual parish-wide collection envelope for altar and sanctuary needs supplements the budget with about another $1,000, which is earmarked for such sanctuary needs as purchasing material for the holy cloths, new finger bowl liners for the holy water fonts, a holy water dispenser, vestments for priests and deacons, and baptismal garment cloths or items that the rector may need help funding. Overall, the group historically has been known for its generosity of time, talent, and treasure to the parish and the world documented in the chapter on social justice. The members overwhelmingly consider themselves important to the parish although some report feeling underappreciated as noted in figure.14. They also self-assess that the society could improve such as recruiting more members seen in figure 15. It is time for a Membership Committee to be reinstituted and it has been. A Publicity Committee to promote membership and visibility would be helpful. The challenge will be to encourage members to participate in this endeavor, that is, to take on leadership roles. These critical issues were discussed at the 10th annual retreat in the summer of 2017, which was dedicated to reflection on the future. Those plans are presented later in this book.

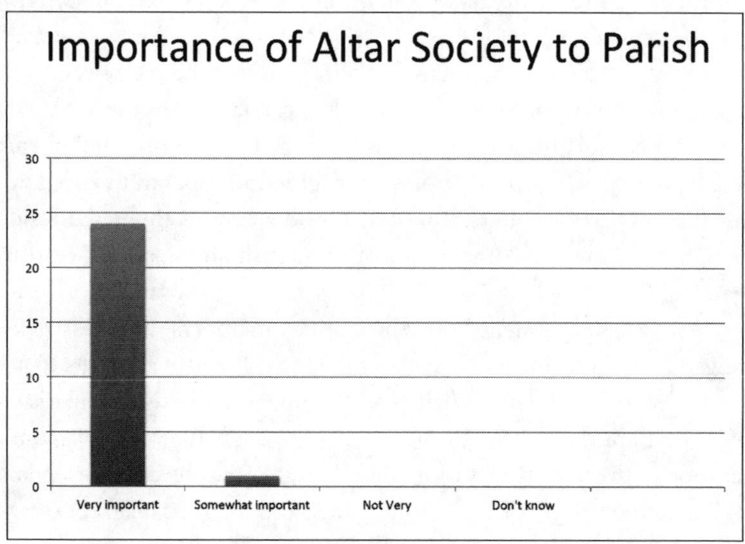

Figure 14

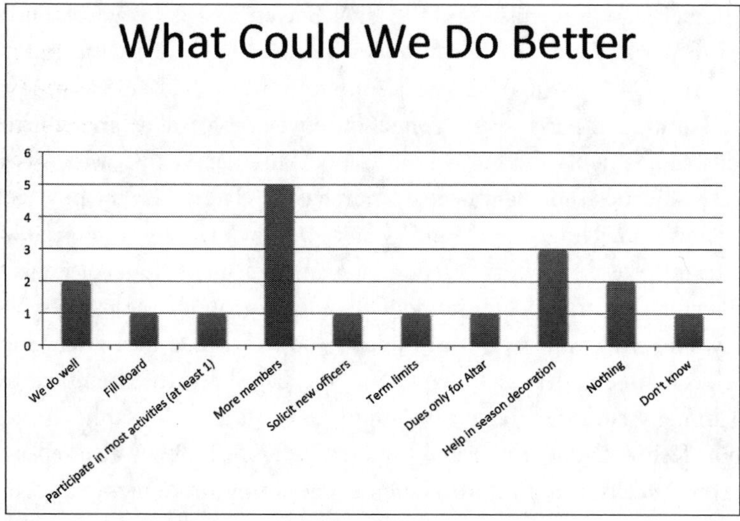

Figure 15

The St. Francis Altar Society does a lot. Some such as mentor Sister Emilia Atencio has said she knows of no other altar society that does so much. A church organizational expert and professor has commented to President Skya Abbate on Skya's analysis of the society that she thinks the society does too much. Yet this is our mission and our structure. It has not only worked for ten decades but has thrived and been deeply meaningful to its members. The Song of Solomon 1:3 reminds us of the invitation to the richness of the oasis of God who is calling. Can we like Solomon respond, "Draw me: We will run."

Christmas Arrangement

4

Flowers

The Symbols of Our Work

"ALL THE FLOWERS OF ALL THE TOMORROWS ARE SEEDS OF TODAY AND SELDOM DO WE REALIZE THAT THE GLORY AND THE POWER OF HIM WHO MADE THE UNIVERSE LIE HIDDEN IN A FLOWER."

Brother Brian, July 1980

FLOWERS IN THE TRADITION

GOLDEN FORSYTHIAS BURSTING FROM the baptismal font in spring, white roses blooming from a crown of thorns at Easter, bare aspens bowing to the altar in Advent—such is the work of the St. Francis Altar Society within the rich Roman Catholic tradition and its longstanding role in connection with liturgy and decoration. Situated within the tri-cultural community of Hispanic, Caucasian, and Native American peoples, the Altar Society honors decorative traditions that are not static but vibrant manifestations of the historical matrix within which the parish exists along with its deep of love of nature.

Jane McAvoy, author of *The Changing Image of Parish Ministry*[1] suggests, "In order to understand the present we must cast a glance backward to the past, for it is from the past that our current images have come." Such institutional insight unveils the importance and the pride that the members of the society have placed upon church environment as a function of their society.

In plumbing their canvass of history, the Altar Society emerges as an effervescent community of ladies whose love of flowers was its crown. It is notable that in 1949, when a new parish school was being built, that the rector of the parish and the Spiritual Director of the Altar Society felt that the $300 a year spent on flowers (which today would buy one Easter arrangement) would be better suited to the funding of the new school. He asked the members to bring flowers from their gardens to adorn the altar and they did! Anecdotal stories relay that the members could be seen making their way across the downtown plaza, cleaning buckets, rags and flowers in tow on their way to care for the church: certainly a humbling sight.

The idea of flowers as central to the church's environment is a deeply held concept in the Altar Society. In the physically dry desert symbolic of our faith we delight in introducing into the liturgical environment the elements, flowers, and colors of creation that honor God and participate in our redemption. The Old Testament expounds, "Her deserts he shall make like Eden, her wasteland like the garden of the Lord." (Isa 51:3) This quote has abundant meaning both literally and symbolically for the Altar Society in the high mountain desert of Santa Fe, New Mexico. Here the women strived for most of the society's existence to make the church environment an Eden. They desired to see their church as a place of beauty, nourishment, repose and delight, at times adorning the altar with the flowers lovingly grown in their own gardens or for almost ninety years paid for by the fundraising of the Altar Society. As former President Emilia Sedillo proudly recounted in 1983, "Every day of the year there were fresh flowers at the altar."

Flowers and Discipleship

If landscape possesses the potential to shape consciousness, then the stark natural beauty of New Mexico allows the unformed soul to mature and expand, develop and transform beyond the interminable blue mountain

1. McAvoy, *Changing*, 65.

skies and native pinons.Its paradoxical ruggedness juxtaposed with the fragility of rarefied mountain air and sparse desert terrain, hones the intellect to discern the essential nature of things, a skill that is indispensable to life, church, and ministry. The high mountain desert offers 360 days of year-round sunshine that alternate through seasons from crisp and clear, to hot and dry.In a geographic area that acutely acknowledges the interdependence of water and earth, we are posed to understand the delicate balance of nature and summon the Altar Society to think about its interdependent, mystical relationships with each other and within the context of the natural world. Its strong historical, rural, and cultural connections with nature, the desert, and flowers form a naturalistic and sacramental framework for how the society interprets what it does. The connection is primal, unequivocal, understated, and somewhat unexplored. This is perhaps part of the reason why the flowers hold such allure for the members of the Altar Society.

This interest in flowers as living tokens that give glory to God has been the longstanding magnet that drew women into the society although interest in serving the church with likeminded women was also part of their motivation to become a member. This appeal is not surprising since in most people's minds the Altar Society is equated with flowers.

However, once members joined the society they quickly learned there were many more functions that the society was charged with performing for the parish and the archdiocese. At that point, each member is challenged to reinterpret their personal interest in the flowers or any other reason they might join and reframe their motivation as a ministerial invitation to service to the altar. To sustain membership, the members must convert their personal aspirations within the society and make their participation integrated, imaginative, and inspired. Discipleship has its challenges!

As one might expect, flower budgets varied with the times and the cost of living but the Cathedral always had flowers that were paid for by the Altar Society fundraisers such as their famous Silver Teas. It was not until the early 2000s that the Liturgy Committee and the parish budgets began to pay for the flowers, thus marking a change in fundraising activities, the dissolution of the long-held Silver Teas, and the women's primary custody of the flowers.

When the Liturgy Committee was formalized in 1998 the Altar Society worked closely with that group as the executors on floral art. Prior to that the Altar Society membership played a vital and independent role in church decoration and flower arrangement for most of its history. In

2012 the society was no longer in charge of flowers. Members of the Liturgy Committee, the Altar Society, and a newly created Art and Environment Committee, augmented by the youth group, are currently involved in preparing and decorating the worship space for the liturgical seasons of the church under the direction of the rector and the Pastoral Associate for Liturgy. This was the role most cherished by the membership, a role that is alive in recent memory, and one that they no longer independently possess today. It is a change that sparks unresolved tension at decorating times and in the minds of those who feel that this task was usurped from the society. Yet the invitation to work in association with the other committees in regard to the flowers is still open to all. In most ways it is better coordinated, leaner yet richer, and less ostentatious or gaudy but as a change it is challenging. Curiously, in 1998, Fr. Emmanuel suggested that only cactus type flowers were suitable for the Blessed Sacrament Chapel, an idea that gratefully has not persisted! The society needs to learn that things change.

Currently and into the foreseeable future, as art ministers and "custodians of the visual imagery of the church"[2], especially with flowers, the aforementioned groups implement seasonal and pastoral visions of creating an appropriate church environment to complement liturgical services. Together, their task is to assist in the critical role of opening up for others the noble simplicity of environment suggested in the liturgical guidelines on art and environment. Depending upon the vision of the particular rector at the time, and his rightful interpretation of decoration and liturgical space, the involvement of the Altar Society may be broad or narrow but it interfaces with the work of the other committees and all are welcome.

Interestingly, church documents only rarely have anything to say about seasonal decoration maintains liturgical writer Peter Mazar in his book *To Crown the Year.*[3] He references *Environment and Art in Catholic Worship (EACW)* by citing, "Whatever the style or type, no art has a right to a place in liturgical celebration if it is not high quality and if it is not appropriate. Because the assembly gathers in the presence of God to celebrate his saving deeds, liturgy's climate is one of awe, mystery, wonder, reverence, thanksgiving and praise. So it *cannot be satisfied with anything less than the Beautiful* in its environment and all its artifacts, movements and appeal to the senses."[4]

2. Mazar, *Crown*, 7.

3. Mazar, *Crown*, 244.

4. *EACW* in Mazar, 7–8.

Built of Living Stones: Art, Architecture, and Worship further describes the broad parameters of floral decoration.

> The tradition of decorating or not decorating the church for liturgical seasons and feasts heightens the awareness of the festive, solemn, or penitential nature of these seasons. Human minds and hearts are stimulated by the sounds, sights, and fragrances of liturgical seasons, which combine to create powerful, lasting impressions of the rich and abundant graces unique to each of the seasons.
>
> Plans for seasonal decorations should include other areas besides the sanctuary. Decorations are intended to draw people to the true nature of the mystery being celebrated rather than being ends in themselves. Natural flowers, plants, wreaths and fabric hangings, and other seasonal objects can be arranged to enhance the primary liturgical points of focus. The altar should remain clear and freestanding, not walled in by massive floral displays or the Christmas crib, and pathways in the narthex, nave, and sanctuary should remain clear.
>
> Objects such as the Advent wreath, and other traditional seasonal appointments proportioned to the size of the space and to the other furnishings can enhance the prayer and understanding of the parish community.
>
> The use of living flowers and plants, rather than artificial greens, serves as a reminder of the gift of life God has given to the human community. Planning for plants and flowers should include not only the procurement and placement but also the continuing care needed to sustain living things.

Since then, in accordance with *The Constitution of the Sacred Liturgy*[5] "it is the sacred task of the art minsters to marry liturgy with floral art by selecting the non-verbal accompaniments and symbols of faith that elicit adoration and praise, new life and sorrow, austerity and glory, in short, decoration must bear the weight and mystery of our ineffable God." This noble simplicity is overall the objective for the environmental space. *Environment and Art in Catholic Worship* additionally implies the nobility of the liturgical space and its connection with flowers when they state, "One should be able to sense something special (and nothing trivial) in everything that is seen and heard, touched and smelled, and tasted in liturgy."[6] In that same document we hear,"While our words and art forms cannot

5. Paul VI, *Constitution of Liturgy*.
6. *EACW* no. 25 in Mazar.

contain or confine God, they can like the world itself, be icons, avenues of approach, numinous presence, ways of touching without totally grasping or seizing." [7] In short, the society is beckoned to become more fluid with the church directives and with each rector's style, and to reinterpret, realign, and resolve the interpretation of service to the altar as the primary reason why the society exists.

As an example, when I became the President in 2005, I also had to do this reinterpretation. The first thing I did was to get rid of all the plastic and silk flowers used by the Altar Society. This corresponded with the *Constitution's* affirmations for noble decoration (#24).[8] Many of the ladies at first thought I was wasteful or that I was criticizing their work but I used my position and my knowledge to explain why the change had occurred. From then on we have adorned the church with real flowers. If I had not done so the future rector would have for plastic flowers do seem to lack "nobility." Since 2012, a new rector has chosen to use more live green plants instead of flowers, which in their "greenness" is suitable for Ordinary Time. Many members and parishioners have had a hard time with this idea.

In that same year I conducted a small survey that asked, "In five years, if you could envision one thing for the parish, what would it be?" One member of the Altar Society wrote, "Since it is a Basilica and tourist attraction, flowers on the altar all of the time. Many tourists have commented on how beautiful it looks and would like to take home ideas from the Basilica to their parishes. I don't think plain keeps your attentiveness to prayer only. It is beautiful to see the Lord's home displayed in all its beauty (Survey Subject A). This insight, while perhaps not practical, affordable, or liturgically appropriate, illustrates the power of the catechesis of flowers as environmental art, the catechesis Brother Brian offered at the start of this chapter.

Through culture, tradition, pre-Vatican II times (Vatican II 1962–1965), and perhaps even an organic awareness of the naturalness of flowers for decoration, the members have become used to flowers by the altar. Today the society with the other committees has expanded and explored the idea of church decoration in liturgy to enhance the faith and worship experience of the parishioners. Reluctantly the group is transitioning from a rather sumptuous use of flowers to more understated nobility. Long-standing ideas take time to unearth perhaps because flowers evoke memories from

7. *EACW* no. 25 in Mazar.

8. Paul VI, *Constitution of Liturgy*, #24.

deep in our core, or childhood memories, and even church history. It is surprising how "red" is so ingrained as the official poinsettia color, vying for a place with the liturgical white. We are challenged to appreciate that perhaps compromises complement each other.

The Role of the Art Minister

As the church documents have illustrated, art ministers have the important role in opening up for others the signs and symbols and the reality of faith with the visual imagery of the season.[9] They play a life-giving role in ministry. "While our words and art cannot contain or confine God, they can like the world itself, be icons, avenues of approach, numinous presence, ways of touching without totally grasping or seizing."[10] The society's viewpoint as women decorators is significant in a church where the feminine tends to be excluded in leadership roles, yet the Altar Society is part of a complementary structure and should continue to participate in decoration through ideas and service, such as through their personal purchase and freedom for flower provisions for First Friday, participation in the Liturgy Committee, and seasonal decoration. Just as God's relationship with us began in the ecological garden so too do we need to repair that fractured relationship brought about by sin by valuing the garden we are invited to care for through the flowers in church that both renew the human relationships and our relationship with God.

There is some freedom within liturgical planning for themes unique to our congregation to be practiced and the floral art to match that liturgy. Music in Spanish, street processions, or Indian dancers are allowed to involve the parish in our unique historical connection with God in New Mexico and elsewhere. Yet the universality of the Mass, Holy Scripture, and the liturgy of the Roman Catholic Church make it possible to worship God in a familiar way.

The annual Native American Liturgy Mass is celebrated with drums and chant. Proud Buffalo Dancers lower their massive heads as they prance in headdresses in front of the altar. The Eagle Dancers' wings bow to the altar in adoration. To behold the animal dancers participating in liturgy is to gain a glimpse of creation and peace enacted in the post-resurrected world. Native American language reflects the Indian assimilation of Catholicism.

9. Mazar, *Crown*, 139.

10. *EACW* no. 25 in Mazar.

On these occasions the Basilica looks different from any time of year. Using environmental motifs the art ministers bundle pine with the corn, and aspen with native grasses, to mimic the natural world's praise of God. While outside the church in the dry near autumn fields the jimson blossoms have morphed into bulbs swelling with new baby gourds growing on top of last year's fragile shells and dried vines. Generations build upon each other in proper self-propagation. The flowers grow quietly, die silently, but when they live even things without ears can hear them.

Liturgical elements for creating the church space in environmental art through flowers, banners, colors and other elements, assist in focusing the lens of faith and conveying through symbols some of the grandeur and the mystery of God. A new challenge that has not been considered adequately is for the decorators in the parish's committees is to pay attention to how the flowers are grown and where they come from to reduce the carbon-imprint on a tender planet and respect the beauty of God's creation.

St. Francis of Assisi, the patron saint of the parish and the society, immortalized the beauty of creation in his *Canticle of the Creatures*, and the Altar Society is humbled to follow him. Francis believed, says his biographer, "It is the nature of all things to praise their creator. Francis may not have had any idea how flowers or rocks would or could do this but he acted on the belief that they could."[11]So too does the Altar Society as it senses the natural world within which we live.

The abundant chamisa changes its pistachio camouflage to cyan yellow amidst matching elecampane sunflowers as the acrid smell of autumn approaches. Transparent breezes waft through the arches of wisteria that bow to the birds in their arms. Other birds alertly sit on top of trees like stars at Christmas surveying the scene until the other family members arrive to play and eat at the feast. Summer stalks of cool lavender sway their scent to hummingbirds and bees and, when exhausted, fall to their knees. The xeriscaped plants promise restraint, "We won't drink too much water." Indigenous grasses control their own growth saying, "We were here first. We can share too." Stray sunflower seeds that took root hide in the mesh of daisies and echinacea, in the hope to give birth before the gardener arrives. Wildflowers bloom for wild animals. Cherry trees full of pink hats going to a wedding tempt the earth to a marriage with the tender sun. The seasons rotate, the trumpet vines sound. The incandescent light and glory of green plants that neither a canvas nor a camera can capture are here for our

11. Niemier, *In the Footsteps*, 169.

pleasure. Wings and blooms have pierced the veil of heaven's gentle king. The desert landscape is no more of a backdrop for wildlife cloaked with petals or feathers than it is a separate environment. We share a living ecosystem bound in green biospirituality. The Altar Society knows this from deep in their historical, spiritual DNA. It is hard for them to be divorced from the flowers.

A flaming red rose by the altar, a spotless white lily beneath the resurrected Christ, heady spider mums dancing by the candles—these are the light of his face, the curved touch of his grace, in the life-giving energy of the natural world. Is it any wonder that the Altar Society loves flowers? Now the members must love the society enough to see that the real flowers for the altar are the fruits of our spirit with which we do that work and that we can share this noble task with others.

Lyle Quintana Johnson Christmas Flower Report, 1980

In all places and in all seasons flowers expand their light, soul-like wings, teaching us by most persuasive reasons how akin they are to human things. So the poinsettia, the flower of the Holy Night, which so beautifully decked the Cathedral this Christmastide to celebrate again this most joyous moment in mankind's history, the birth of the infant Savior, the Child of the Holy Night.

The lovely custom of having fresh flowers began in the tenth century when Georg Jacob, an Arabian geographer, wrote the legend of the blossoming trees. According to the story, on the night that Christ was born, all of the trees in the forest bloomed and bore fruit. Quickly, the legend spread across Europe, until today, in many lands, the plant kingdom celebrates Christmas with fresh flowers.

In the United States, of course, the poinsettia is the traditional Christmas flower, though really, it is much too recent an immigrant to our country, to be called traditional. Joel Poinsett, our minster to Mexico, introduced the first plants to the United States in 1828. He planted them in his own gardens and shared the increase with his neighbors. But it wasn't until the early 1900s that it became a popular Christmas flower.

In Mexico where it is known as *"Flor de la noche buena,"* "Flower of the Holy Night," there are numerous legends that attempt to explain its popularity. One of the prettiest is about a child in Cuernavaca who wept because she had no flowers to place in the manger at Christmas. An angel appeared to her and directed her to pick a weed, place it at the altar and wait. The child obeyed and the weed was transformed into a lovely plant bearing the whorl of scarlet leaves.

From the dramatic flame leaf of the poinsettia to the delicate Christmas rose, from great boughs of holly to small sprigs of mistletoe, nature's own Christmas ornament outshining even the grandest of those modern-day, contribute to make our winter holidays the most beautiful of the year.

The poinsettias furnished this Christmas by The Flower Nook amounted to $300.00, but with a discount of one-third, the cost to the altar society came to $200.00. Incidentally, the wreath and spray decorations were a contribution by The Flower Nook, something they have done for years.

Photos by Josh Estey/The New Mexican

Tessie Anchondo places a cloth over the altar at St. Francis Cathedral. Anchondo is one of three woman who clean the church altar.

Figure 17 Linens for the Lord

5

The Years

The Call to the Altar

"It is the duty of every Catholic woman to be a member of her parish altar society."

Fr. Cletus, Rector and Spiritual Director, 1952

OVERVIEW

In this chapter, several short histories of the St. Francis Altar Society, augmented by a long analysis of the latter years are captured and organized into one historical narrative. Those years included 1921 to 1964, 1964 to 1974, 1975 to 1977, 1978 to 1982, 1983 to 1988 and a broad overview from 1921 to 1990. No summary was made after 1990, a period of almost thirty years! One of the purposes of this book is to continue the tradition of recording the history, not only for these missing years but also for the entire history of the Altar Society. Furthermore, this undertaking offers a broad panorama of the work of the society as a unique ministry mostly of women in the Roman Catholic Church in Santa Fe, New Mexico, New Mexico's oldest city from 1607,[1] the 3rd oldest city and the oldest state capital in the United States.[2]

In looking back, most churches in the 1960s had altar societies and it was common for many women to belong to one.[3] As Father Cletus of the Cathedral thought, it was an obligation. However, today in a parish like the Cathedral Basilica of St. Francis of Assisi, many mothers work, college kids are away, and the regional Catholic school is on the opposite end of town where many families have relocated to from the downtown area. Women, mostly in their 60s and 70s, and virtually all retired, make up the current membership.

Thousands of pages of minutes begin in 1947 and endure through the present. Individually they are business records. Yet when dissected and assimilated they tell a story that is less perfunctory and more thought provoking. The members of the Spiritual Development and Writing Club who helped write this book read and studied all those minutes and have noted what they considered to be the salient features of those years. Brief historical events that the members themselves recounted are included for contextualization and are integrated into those time spans to tell a chronological story.

In the subsequent chapter, the Presidents, the history is also told from the perspectives of the annual reports of the Presidents, supplemented with interviews with the eight living Presidents. Thus, the extensive history of the St. Francis Altar Society speaks in a multidimensional voice heard from its histories, minutes, reports, interviews and writers. As an interesting historical note, over 175 announcements, full-fledged articles, and delightful photos about the society and its meetings, priests, events and especially the Silver Teas were found in the *Santa Fe New Mexican*, the local newspaper, from 1956 to 1970. This coverage perhaps reflects the nature of news at the time and as well as the Catholicity of the city.

1. *The 10 Oldest Cities.*
2. *Oldest State Capital.*
3. Langlois, *Parish Altar Societies.*

THE HISTORY FROM 1921 TO 2018

Freedom, War, and the Laundry from 1921 to 1959 —the First 30 Years

On November 16, 1964, Mrs. Clara Sweeney, assisted by Clara Moehn, submitted a four-page report, the earliest history of the St. Francis Altar Society, stemming from 1921 to 1964. In that account they referenced the information found in the Mission chapter of this book on the founding of the society, its mission and activities such as care for the altar and church, the sewing and mending of the linens, and the spiritual and charitable activities of the members. Of the original 55 charter members, 11 were living at this time and were still members of the Altar Society 43 years later.

In its relative infancy during the 1930s, the Altar Society became affiliated with the National Council of Catholic Women, and its local branch, the Archdiocesan Council of Catholic Women. Four Altar Society members served as Archdiocesan Presidents and two members served on the national board. Membership dues were ten cents per month. A penny collection was taken up at the meetings, and during World War II (1939–1945) was used to buy war stamps. Members also participated in a Radio Rosary Crusade during the war.

On the 25th anniversary of the society in 1946, a Valentine tea was held to honor the living charter members. Ten years later, on the 35th anniversary in 1956, another tea was celebrated at the St. Francis Center. That year members assisted at an open house for the Order of the Carmelite nuns when the sisters established their monastery in Santa Fe. Throughout its history that peaceful location has served as a spiritual sanctuary for many and a place where the Altar Society has had Masses said for ill and deceased members from that time to the present.

A particularly nostalgic image that captures the spirit and devotion of the women in this era was the familiar sight of Mrs. Joseph Moya. In the days before automobile transportation, the history notes she could be seen "walking to the Cathedral early on Saturday morning, scrub pail and cleaning equipment in hand. In the summer she usually carried a bouquet of flowers from her own garden."

In 1947, clothing, towels, and soap were collected for the destitute in Europe following World War II. Internally, the Altar Society made a decision that no special collections or requests for donations other than those directly sponsored by the society could be permitted at any meeting in order to conserve funds and to meet the needs of the society. Members held their monthly meeting at the Catholic Maternity center on the corner of Delgado Street and Palace Avenue. Abroad in England, Queen Elizabeth and Prince Philip wed.

In 1948, the first of two "Freedom Trains," traveled throughout the United States and arrived in Santa Fe. Their purpose was to remind all that freedom cannot be taken for granted. The exhibit featured priceless national treasures that celebrate American Liberty, along with documents of tyranny and despotism. They included the Bill of Rights, the Constitution, the Gettysburg Address, the Magna Carta, and many other American documents to show to people who might never get to see them in Washington, D.C.[4] [5]

That year dues rose from $1.00 to $1.50. The laundry, always an issue with the society, was now done by the Sisters of St. Mary's Convent for a fee of $30 a month. A suggestion was made to have the Spiritual Director attend the meetings on occasion and so the members decided to discuss this with Fr. Cletus the rector. Six dollars were allocated out of the general fund to purchase First Friday flowers for adoration. Constitutional changes recorded in the chapter on the Mission were instituted and included a monthly low Mass for all living and deceased members.

The charity of the society was central to their practices. From the Catholic Clinic, to the Christmas money, to the Catholic Maternity Institute, and the clothes made by the Altar Society members for children, many groups were gifted. In cooperation with the Santa Fe Archdiocese Council of Women, a baby shower was held to collect clothes for the needy of Europe in war devastated countries. Additionally, funds were allocated for the church. For example, the society contributed money towards kneelers in the main church and a rug for the sanctuary.

In 1949, a set of dishes was designed for Altar Society functions. The setting consisted of a dinner plate, a bread plate, a small bowl, and a coffee cup and saucer made of white china trimmed in gold and inscribed, "St. Francis Altar Society Santa Fe, New Mexico."

When the price of flowers for the church amounted to $300 a year, with the typical Easter flower bill of $56.00, Fr. Cletus serving as Spiritual Director suggested that the money be better spent to furnish the parochial

4. *Freedom Train.*

5. *America Freedom Train.*

school. As a result, the flowers were no longer purchased by the society but provided by the members' gardens. The Sisters of the parish did the laundry of the linens, which they claimed was a big job!At the time, Msgr. George Reiffer borrowed some linens for use at the seminary by some visiting priests and the scrupulous Sisters promptly sent him the bill!!

Concern for those ravaged by the war continued. Swan soap wrappers were collected which had some trade-in value along with 80 bars of laundry soap, 21 bars of toilet soap, and Thanksgiving clothing donations. The women were happy to report, "A lot of nice clothing for the war relief was brought in." The parish was encouraged by the Santa Fe District to draw the membership of all women of the parish into these efforts in the aftermath of the war.

Interestingly, a Spanish Altar Society coexisted along with the St. Francis Altar Society going back to approximately 1940. Reference is made in the 1949 minutes that the two Altar Societies merged to decrease the cost of dues in participating in the national organization. The remaining Spanish document, *Reglamento,* is fascinating small pamphlet on their mission, rules, and procedures which were considerably different from the St. Francis Altar Society. It can be consulted in the chapter on Mission.

A recommendation was made to meet in a new hall, the St. Francis Catholic Center, at the intersection of Alameda Street and Palace Avenue, but the members chose to meet monthly at each other's homes. The Altar Society compiled recipes and sold cookbooks for $1.00 each. At the end of the year an Altar Society hostess played the organ during the Christmas social to the delight of the members.

In 1950, clothing was needed for the Pope's storerooms for refugees and Mrs. Frank Ortiz y Davis and Miss Clara Berchtold received the papal cross from the Pope. Unfortunately, nothing more could be discovered about the Pope's storerooms or the papal cross. Clothes were collected for the local Larragoite School. The Sisters of Saint Mary's Convent stopped doing the laundry and Fr. Cletus' housekeeper took over and they were "beautifully done" but not for long!

Sadly, an Indian rug and side altar cover were stolen from the church in 1951. The Altar Society decided to host a spaghetti dinner to raise money and replace them. The cost of the meal would be $1.25 for adults and $0.75 cents for children. Due to the high cost of food the dinner had to be cancelled. In lieu of the dinner each member decided to donate $2.00, which was a lot of money at the time to replace the missing items. Thanksgiving prayers were offered for much needed snow.

Fr. Cletus embraced his position as the society's Spiritual Director and was involved with the Altar Society and its functions. In 1952, he wanted the Altar Society to participate in the Civil Defense efforts because the "Altar Society was very charitable." He observed that the Altar Society is made up of "Marthas and Marys" and commended the Martha part very highly by praising the way the altar, linens, and sewing were looked after. But he said there was room for improvement in the Mary part of the society. He suggested that more spiritual benefits could be gained by setting aside a Sunday when the society could go to communion as a body as they had done in other years. Also, he suggested that members could go in groups or in a body on First Fridays to adore the Blessed Sacrament. He felt that the society should promote sociability among other Catholic women by having the Membership Committee or the Hospitality Committee call all women in the parish and impress upon them that "It is the duty of every Catholic woman to be a member of her parish Altar Society."

During this period early childhood nutrition needed addressing close to home. The local Women's Club solicited money for cans of milk for children under the age of one. Seven cans per week for total of $1,500 per year were required to assist 98 percent of the needy who were also Catholic. The Altar Society members were asked to bring one can of milk to each meeting to help these children and their families.

During the post-war years, it was incumbent upon the government to provide information on what would happen in case of atomic disaster and so the women received that information. Civil Defense registration forms were also distributed so the women could offer their services.

This year the ladies used artificial poinsettias to adorn the altar at Christmas and they were proud of them. When it was discovered that the Altar Society china was used by other groups the ladies petitioned Fr. Cletus to put a lock on their cabinet. With his curious logic he believed that a lock would invite further vandalism so the ladies were admonished to keep the china somewhere else.

In 1953, Fr. Cletus continued to postulate, "A good parish cannot exist without the help of the women." Two women dutifully took care of the altar every Saturday and on special occasions. Fr. Cletus suggested a holy hour vigil every First Friday and the women found that favorable. The laundress was now complaining about the amount of linens to wash and iron!

The Altar Society continued its community outreach and collected Catholic magazines for the prisoners at the State Penitentiary. When St. Vincent's Orphanage faced closing in 1954 the women appealed it. At this time, Dwight D. Eisenhower was President.

In 1955, Fr. Pax Schicker, the new rector, was introduced to the society. He told the women that it was a great honor to care for the altar and recognizing their value said he would co-operate with the activities of the society and he hoped the women would continue their work.

Discussion about the pros and cons of fluoridation of water happened on the national level. The Altar Society now assumed the custody of the laundry and some of the members were paid to do it.

To publicize the work of the Altar Society prayer cards were distributed. In 1957, Fr. Pax asked the ladies to make three dozen surplices for the altar boys in a short period of time so the ladies hustled. Continuing their work in social justice, in 1958, the Altar Society sent Christmas cards to hospitalized disabled veterans. To mourn the passing of Pope Pius XII, the Altar Society Sewing Committee made surplices and drapes for the local Cathedral service.

In contrast to today's practices, no refreshments were served during Lent at the Altar Society meetings in 1959. Transportation was arranged for members to come to the meetings if they required it. Mrs. Johnson complained,"The organ is too loud," and Fr. Pax took care of it! Meetings continued to be held in the members' homes. The ever-present issue of linens persisted and now a woman was paid to do the ironing. The voluntary penny collection amounted to $1.92 and the ladies were pleased with this generosity. The aforementioned Spanish Altar Society was invited to attend the next meeting at the Catholic Clinic and to join in Corporate Communion. A footrest for the confessional was purchased for Fr. Pax.

Times of Unrest, Celebration, and Flourishing from 1960–1990—the Middle Years

A milestone Post Office box was acquired in 1960. Fr. Pax requested a report from the Altar Society on what he considered their good works so he could incorporate it into his annual report. He continued to request that many women who were not members be called and invited to the Altar Society.

In 1961, Father Pax continued his spiritual direction and beseeched the Altar Society to pray for the elderly, especially those who were confined to their homes or nursing homes. The next year, Father Pax grilled a steak dinner only for the Altar Society members and topped it off with his special steak sauce! Always in support of the women, he commended the Altar Society for the work they were doing and expressed his pleasure in the reports he had requested that recounted that the society was cooperating and working with each other.

In 1963, a collection for clothes for the orphanage close to the Cathedral was made. In an unforgettable moment President John F. Kennedy was assassinated and Lyndon B. Johnson assumed this weighty post. Longest standing treasurer Olinda Garcia graduated from high school! A year later, in 1964, the Beatles came to the United States and appeared on the Ed Sullivan Show, forever changing American culture. Boxer Cassius Clay changed his name to Muhammad Ali. A Soviet cosmonaut achieved the first space walk now enlarging peoples' perspectives.

In 1964, Clara Sweeney, Historian, wrote another history encompassing 1964–1974 and she presented her report at the January 1976 Altar Society meeting. During this ten-year period she rightly notes that the structural foundation of the society and its achievements remained significantly the same, with an emphasis on the care of the altar and sanctuary, the spiritual development of its members, and involvement in community action and world responsibility.

In 1965, Reverend Martin Luther King Jr. was arrested in Selma, Alabama, Malcolm X was shot to death, and Winston Churchill died. Adoration of the Blessed Sacrament continued without interruption on First Fridays but there was less interest in retreats. The Corporate Communions were discontinued due to lack of participation but were then reinstated and well attended later in 1974. Joseph I. Butler, whose wife Dottie Butler was the President of the Altar Society in 1966, was the manger of the Interstate Laundry and La Linda Laundry. He generously donated free linen service to the Altar Society for approximately five years in an unparalleled and appreciated gesture.

In connection with their practice of world responsibility, in 1967, 18 ditty bags were assembled for soldiers who were patients in Veterans' hospitals. This project continued for several years. The members also formed a short-lived study group on international relations with South America. Monthly contributions continued for the local Villa Therese Clinic that offered free medical care to residents near the Cathedral. The members made weekly visits to nursing homes and took a blind woman to confession and Mass. A woman was hired to clean the altar for $5 a week under Elsie Haake. Stunningly, three astronauts were killed during a test launch in the United States.

Two more scars were etched upon American life when Americans mourned their losses with the assassinations of Martin Luther King Jr. on April 4, 1968 and Senator Robert F. Kennedy on his campaign to be the Democratic nominee for President on June 5, 1968. When he died on June 6, much of the hope that he engendered for the poor, Blacks, and the average person died with him. Just two years earlier the Civil Rights Act, designed to eliminate discrimination, had been signed into law.

To ease the sting of loneliness and ostracism Christmas packages were provided to American soldiers during the Vietnam War (1954–1975) in 1970 and money was given to the Red Cross. Corporate Communions were still held once a month. It was a period when notices of the Altar Society meetings appeared in the *New Mexican*, on radio, and in the Cathedral bulletin.

The Annual Silver Tea was held at U.S. Congressman Joseph Montoya and his wife Della's home. The next Silver Tea followed at Governor Jerry Apodaca and his wife Clara's residence. Both Della and Clara were members of the Altar Society.

A highlight of this period was the Golden Jubilee of the Altar Society. In 1971, 76 members celebrated it with a luncheon at the *La Posada* Inn. Here, they honored the 20 living Presidents and Fr. Austin Ernestes. In reference to the selfless devotion and the time consuming work to properly maintain the society, truly a labor of love, Father Austin remarked,"It is surely recorded in heaven." A simple 50th jubilee song, was crafted to the tune of "Happy Birthday." While not an opera all could sing along! It goes as follows:

Happy jubilee for us
Happy jubilee for us
Happy jubilee dear members
Happy jubilee for us.
May the Holy Spirit enlighten us
May the Holy Spirit enlighten us
Happy jubilee dear members
Happy jubilee for us

According to President Margaret Bindel, 1971 was a year of spiritual formation of members, friendliness, and corporal works of mercy. In 1972, a Spiritual Formation Committee and members prayed the rosary. Retreat Mass cards were made. Sympathy cards were sent to members' families. The Friendly Visitor Committee visited the sick and the leprosy missions were supported. President Mary Reese reminded the members in 1974, "What could be sweeter than to serve the altar?"

1975 commemorated the 100th anniversary of the Archdiocese of Santa Fe, 125 as a diocese, and 350 years since the arrival of *La Conquistadora* in 1625. To mark the events, the Society President donated prayer cards and stationary to the society. Father Austin, who had been the Spiritual Director for many years, was transferred to another parish. Father Reynaldo Rivera became the new Spiritual Director and Lyle Quintana Johnson the next President. The society's china, which had been used in the past for many functions and then moved because it could not be locked up per Fr. Cletus, was found in a storage room! The society then managed to sell 21 sets out of 50 for $2.50 each.

In 1976, the United States celebrated its bicentennial and rededicated itself to the ideas upon which it had been founded. The society purchased vestments and albs for the Franciscan Friars, along with altar boy robes, a beautiful cloth for the Blessed Sacrament altar, liners for the holy water fonts and material for corporals. It was noted that Rose Fidel made "some lovely red satin stoles with crosses embroidered on them for our membership Corporate Communion."

Virgina Wicks, Historian, composed a short history from 1975 to 1977 to keep the tradition of history writing alive. She wrote, "Many varied and multi-colored events, innovations and changes have shaped the history of our Altar Society for the years 1975, 1976 and 1977, during which time Lyle Quintana Johnson was the society president, and during which time our membership increased and we experienced spiritual, cultural and material growth as well."

The members voted in 1977 to withhold $60 or more from the Easter and Christmas flower collections to provide flowers throughout the year for the Blessed Sacrament Chapel. Additionally, Mela Martin, sister to Concha Ortiz y Pino de Kleven, personally arranged to purchase flowers for the Blessed Sacrament altar for one year.

At the end of this period, 3 of the charter members still were members of the society. Virginia beautifully concluded and summarized an ideal that could still be invoked today. She prayed, "May God continue to enfold us in his love, to divinely bless our aims and endeavors, to guide us, and to strengthen us as we continue learning together in love, working together in love and growing together in love as members of the St. Francis Altar Society."

In 1977, monthly meetings were still in the members' homes and at the Inn of the Governors. The membership was growing to the point that it was difficult to have meetings in the members' homes. Dues increased from $6 to $10. A change in the Constitution was also made that "The Constitution of this Society may be amended only by a 2/3 vote of those present, provided that the proposed amendment has been read at two previous meetings."

In 1978, Historian Mary Reese typed on crunchy onionskin paper that most of what was accomplished by the society was a continuation of the mission of the society since it was founded in 1921. Lyle Johnson's famous meditations were presented at liturgically appropriate months and illustrated by "her fabulous collection of antique religious art of Europe, Mexico, Latin America and the primitive folk art of New Mexico." The unsold dinnerware was given to some needy families who were delighted to have it!

Hulda Sellingsloh and Clorinda Garcia designed the first Altar Society banner. On red satin with gold braids and fringe, the crossed arms inspired by the Franciscan shield symbolized the union of Christ and St. Francis of Assisi. It was first displayed at the third Sunday Corporate Communion on May 18, 1978 and now hangs in the hall of the sacristies along with the banners of other ministries.

In 1979, the care of the linens was given to a local laundry. Lyle Quintana Johnson's meditations on the lives of the saints were often read at the meetings. Mother Theresa (now St. Theresa of Calcutta) won the Nobel Peace Prize while at home the 3-mile island nuclear accident occurred. Artistic displays were brought to the Altar Society's meetings in lieu of the Spiritual Director's lack of attendance. The 3rd Sunday of the month Corporate Communions continued.

Rest homes for the elderly that housed Altar Society members were visited in 1980. Christmas flower money was collected in decorated baskets at the main entrance of the church at the end of Mass. At World Community Day, Catholic attendance was the highest ever but the Presbyterians outnumbered all the others!

Tragically in 1980, a riot at the Penitentiary of New Mexico in Santa Fe broke out, one that is without parallel in the penal history of the United States for its brutality, destruction, and the disorganization among the rioters. After a day and a half order was forcefully restored but during that time, 7 of the 12 correctional officers were beaten or sexually violated, 33 inmates were killed by other inmates, 12 were first tortured and mutilated, and 200 were beaten and raped. A crucifix that survived the fire at the prison now hangs in the Blessed Sacrament Chapel at the Cathedral. Beatle John Lennon was murdered outside his home in New York. Ronald Regan was President. The Cathedral parish meeting room in the back of the Cathedral became the new meeting place for the members. 1981 marked the 800th anniversary of St. Francis of Assisi!

At the World Day of Prayer the Altar Society had the largest attendance and was given the White Dove Award. On August 5, 1982 beloved pastor Father Reynaldo Rivera was slain on what seemed to be a sick call to a home south of Santa Fe near Waldo. Thousands attended his funeral as the bell tower swallows swooped, "Good goodbye, and Good night." His murder is a case that is still unsolved to this day. He had recently celebrated his silver jubilee as a priest in 1978. Later, in 1983, a joint proclamation of the New Mexico Legislature honored Father Reynaldo Rivera in the wake of his untimely death.

The beautiful glass panels with etchings depicting the 12 apostles were installed in the Blessed Sacrament Chapel and greatly improved the appearance of this special chapel for all who worshipped there. Mary Reese wrote that she believed it was an honor to belong to the St. Francis Altar Society and to serve our Lord and his church in this way. An added bonus was the friendly fellowship among the members. Emilia Sedillo commented that fresh flowers adorned the altar every day of the year. Although this may not be liturgically true, it was a lasting impression.

In 1984, the new tradition of making baptismal garments began under Fr. Crispin, now the rector. He asked the Altar Society to make some small baptismal bibs embroidered with red crosses for all the infant baptisms at the parish. Unbeknownst to most including the parents of the infants, this a work that has silently continued to this day, financed by Altar Society membership dues and lovingly cut and designed by the handicraft of the women. This little white garment is a precious symbol of the dignity bestowed in Baptism and entry into the life of Christ. Facetiously, Anna Mae Vigil whined that she had the blisters to prove all the hard work that went into cutting out the little altar robes! Likewise, the altar railing was lovingly cleaned by hand and "helps keep us nice and trim." Piles of Christmas gifts were showered upon the State Hospital in Las Vegas, New Mexico.

At the meeting in 1985 it was announced that blind member Pauline Gomez was recognized as one of Santa Fe's Living Treasures for her contribution to the community as a kindergarten teacher. She was also a reader at the Cathedral. The Corporate Communions continued with an average of 16 ½ people! Thanks were given to the members and "all their mothers who taught them to never say no to what is asked of them."

1986 marked the Centennial Celebration of the Cathedral when it was re-dedicated as the Mother Church of the Santa Fe Archdiocese. 1986 also marked the Altar Society's 65th anniversary. Mayor Louis Montano proclaimed February 16 as St. Francis Altar Society Day and a plaque was bestowed upon the society. The members formed a long procession on entering the church for the anniversary Mass and took their seats up front. Clorinda Garcia won a contest for her drawing of St. Francis depicted herein. The Carmelite nuns hand-painted the priests' vestments.

Figure 18 Clorinda's Francis

Helen noted in 1987 there was hope that then Pope John Paul II, (now St. John Paul II) might visit Santa Fe. Unfortunately, his huge jet could not land at the small Santa Fe airport and car travel from Albuquerque to Santa Fe posed too much of a security problem. However, as he flew overhead in the clear blue sky he spoke on the radio, praising Santa Fe's faith in God and the beauty of the land. He prayed, "God bless New Mexico and all of you." Busloads of New Mexico Catholics then went to see him when he visited Phoenix, Arizona.

In 1988, honoring the death of Archbishop James Peter Davis, the 9th archbishop of Santa Fe, 10 Altar Society members served as the honor guards to the casket the day before the funeral. Archbishop Davis was instrumental in instituting many important changes in what were challenging times in the church. His accomplishments included the restoration of the deaconate and greater participation of Catholics in ecumenical activities.

In 1989, Father Crispin told the members of the need for Pastoral Councils. Rachel Cunningham volunteered to be the first Altar Society representative to the Pastoral Council. In 1990 the parish sacristan of 30 years duration, Della Garcia, was honored with a luncheon.

Times of Social Justice, Scandal, and Adaptation from 1990 to 2018 —the Latter Years

On February 18, 1991, Altar Society Historian Helen June Wheeler condensed the eighty-year history of the St. Francis Altar Society from 1921 to 1990 in a two-page report. She credits the aforementioned records of historians Clara Sweeney and especially those of Mary Reese for the information she used in her report similar in scope to the very first history. Helen wrapped up her report commenting on how the society keeps busy with receptions for incoming and outgoing Franciscans and Annual Silver Teas.

The New Mexico State Hospital in Las Vegas, one of the society's annual projects, was given gifts while Maria Sifuentes and her family made the delivery of clothing to St. Michael's Mission in Arizona in 1990. The family was amazed at how large the mission was.

In 1991, the society collected money for the American Leprosy Mission and saved it in the Leprosy Pig named Francesco. Gifts for the state hospital continued, and President Pat Gonzales' brother delivered them to the patients. He related, "The gifts made them so happy, it was if we had given them a million dollars." He walked out of there so proud that our group had made so many people happy. The Silver Tea was held with Alice King, the Governor's wife, at the Governor's mansion and the annual Altar Society luncheon was replaced by a December brunch.

In 1992, 2,000 pounds of clothing were collected by the women and delivered to the mission center in Arizona by Maria Sifuentes and her family. There the clothes were put up for sale and the money went to the needs of the mission. Locally, gifts for the elderly were delivered to Meadow Home, a nursing facility. The church kneeler cloth was replaced and paid for by the society. Corporate Communion Mass attendance was in another downward cycle.

The Altar Society banner and sign up list was placed in the Blessed Sacrament Chapel for First Fridays in 1983. New Archbishop Michael J. Sheehan was appointed. Christmas gifts continued to be delivered to the Las Vegas Medical Center. A parish rosary was held every Monday and each ministry took one month at a time to lead it. This year when St. Michael's Mission in Arizona petitioned the Altar Society for continued assistance the society concluded that they needed to help others locally thus ending that special ministry.

1994 was the beginning of painful years for the Roman Catholic Church and a difficult test of faith for many. Lawsuits were filed against New Mexican priests in the clergy scandals and the Cathedral had to pay for many of them. The Altar Society assisted in tuition for students and made the priests' vestments. Members at Corporate Communions proudly wore their red stoles until Fr. Cyril told them only priests and deacons wear stoles!He suggested that nametags or medals be worn. Baptismal garments continued to be cut and hand embroidered by members. Due to the rising cost of flowers, florists bid for the commissions.

Juan Martinez, husband to member Mary Jane Martinez, began his studies to become a Deacon in 1996. Mary Jane started assembling a scrapbook on the Silver Teas and other Altar Society news from which some information for this book is gleaned. 1996 marked the 75th anniversary of the society. At the Mass Mary Jane read a history to the congregation. The beautiful new and enduring Stations of the Cross, rendered in a *Santero* style were installed at the cost of $50,000. The new Public Address system was also installed for the same amount of money.

In 1997, a three-year contract was signed by the provincial with the Archdiocese of Santa Fe for the Franciscans to continue to operate the Cathedral until the year 2000. Fr. Sal Aragon made the recommendation to the society that simple but colorful flowers be selected for Easter decorations. He thought that sometimes the flowers became too ostentatious because all the money that was collected went into purchasing as many flowers as there was money. But the members wanted to do it their way. They have always loved their flowers yet other perspectives have value.

Interestingly Fr. Manuel requested in 1998 that only cactus type flowers be put in the Blessed Sacrament Chapel thus illustrating an example of a rector's prerogative and ideas about floral art.The scrapbook that Mary Jane was working on was made available for the membership to view.

On December 28, 1999, after a 79-year tenure, the Franciscan friars left the Cathedral. A part of Cathedral history changed forever but the Franciscan influence remains indelible. Deacon Juan Martinez was ordained that year.

A farewell reception was held for the beloved Franciscans, and Fr. Jerome Martinez y Alire was welcomed as the new rector in 2000. He was presented with a notebook that contained information pertinent to the society and perhaps this contributed to his great love for the Altar Society. Surely all new rectors will be given a copy of this book. He thanked the society for his warm welcome and stated that he was ours—heart, body, and soul.

In a practical endeavor, an Altar Society Collection Envelope was enacted by Fr. Jerome to provide the Altar Society with funding for the copious flowers needed to adorn the Cathedral yearly along with other needs. A Constitutional amendment moved the Altar Society meetings from Monday to Wednesday to interface with Fr. Jerome's schedule. Katherine Drexel, former heiress, founder of a religious order and St. Catherine's Boarding School in Santa Fe was canonized as the second American born saint.

The beautiful new baptismal font was uniquely conceived and constructed in the center of the church in 2001 as the heart of liturgical life. It won best in liturgical design in 2002. Sr. Emilia Atencio, Sister of St. Dominic, was hired as a part-time sacristan, Mass Coordinator, and assistant to pontifical liturgies and was an active member of the society. She is now an Honorary member of the Altar Society; a special friend, and mentor to many. The Friends of the Cathedral were organized to raise funds for the Cathedral and the regional Catholic school.

In this same year Cardinal Bernard Law of Boston resigned due to the clergy sexual abuse scandal that began to characterize a tragic and persistent era in the Catholic Church. Arlene Sisneros painted the colorful and illustrative Altar screen for the Blessed Sacrament Chapel depicting scenes in the life of St. Joseph in 2003. The sidewalks and doors were remodeled. Seven died in the Space Shuttle Columbia accident. Saddam Hussein was captured and the Iraq War began (2003–2011).

In 2004, membership fees increased from $10 to $15. The St. Francis and Cristo Rey schools merged and the *Santo Niño* Regional Catholic School opened. Sanctuary tables were purchased by the society. At this time there were some men in the society and they helped with carrying the heavy Altar Society banner in parish wide processions.

A milestone year, 2005, followed. Fr. Jerome became Monsignor and he celebrated 30 years in the priesthood. Skya Abbate was elected to become most the longstanding President in the Altar Society's history. The Cathedral was elevated to a Basilica, *Santo Niño* Regional Catholic School was dedicated, and Sr. Emilia celebrated her 50th jubilee as a sister. The Tipton Foundation underwrote $250,000.00 for the refurbishing of the original stained-glass windows brought from France in the early 1880s that depict the apostles.

The baptismal garments were now embroidered by a digital sewing machine by member Siiri Sanchez, and members continue to cut them out. Bina Said, owner of Azar rugs, made a substantial donation of beautiful Persian rugs for the sanctuary. The Altar Society helped with the purchases of new church pews. Skya Abbate asked the Altar Society to help the Sacred Heart League, which is a very small group, with the funding for the altar breads. The society decided to pay half of the yearly cost of the hosts at a total of $900 for each group. The society did this for a number of years until it became cost prohibitive for them.

Archbishop Michael J. Sheehan told Monsignor Jerome that he was very complementary of all the Altar Society work from the Chrism Mass through to the May crowning in 2007. The Altar Society sponsored the *Semana Santa* (Holy Week) meal for the parish. It was the 200th anniversary of Rosario Chapel where *La Conquistadora* spends her novena week. Deacon William Kollasch, husband to member Angie Kollasch, celebrated 10 years as a deacon and the Altar Society presented him with a stole as a gift.

In 2008, the Treasures of Wisdom, a ministry of women who honor the history of our church, were formed under the direction of Fr. Oscar Coelho and he served as their chaplain. The *Quarto Centenario* Cathedral Steering committees were formed for the opening and closing events of the

Cathedral's 400th anniversary from October 4, 2009 to August 15, 2010. It was also the 25th anniversary of Archbishop Michael J. Sheehan.

This year, due to the workload and the interest of the women, President Skya Abbate suggested that the Altar and Sanctuary Committee have two groups, one that cleans, and one that does the linens. This way members could choose a way to help with these large tasks. The members adopted the idea and for now the structure is working well. A curious history of the linens is provided retrospectively at the end of this chapter as insight into managing tasks with grace and humor.

The Altar Society began participation in feeding the homeless at the Interfaith Shelter in 2009. Skya Abbate, President, was put in charge of purchasing a new tabernacle. She selected one depicting the Lamb of God, crafted in Spain, for the Blessed Sacrament Chapel. She raised $32,000 from Fr. Bob Lussier and $50 from Siiri Sanchez to pay for it. Unexpectedly, the Altar Society name was eliminated on the Flower Collection Envelope, an act that has caused dissatisfaction in the Altar Society to this day. The money now goes to the financial office. The society then receives half of the money collected to be used for sanctuary needs and no longer needs to purchase the flowers, a job they have done for 88 years since their founding! This change in function fundamentally altered the society's identity, membership, and the interpretation of its ministry.

The newly renovated parish office was dedicated to slain Fr. Reynaldo Rivera. The life-sized Gib Singleton bronze Stations of the Cross were installed on loan for 25 years and positioned in the parish garden. New church bells were installed. Planning for the 400th anniversary continued. A movie was shown on Santa Fe's Catholicism at the Lensic Theater.

Beloved Fr. Oscar Coelho left the parish on reassignment in 2010. The Stations of the Cross Garden was dedicated. It was the 400th anniversary of the Cathedral!

In 2011, the new Roman Missal and Creed were introduced. The Altar Society held a Christmas party at the Interfaith Shelter and served Frito pies and *biscochitos* along with presents of stuffed animals, and gift bags. Everyone helped decorate the Christmas tree. Beloved Pope John Paul II was beatified, and the royal wedding of Prince William and Kate Middleton took place. On the spot, the members donated $985 for the Japan relief fund following a tsunami and nuclear disaster.

In 2012, President Skya Abbate composed a "beautiful and special prayer" for the society to be read at the start of each meeting. Fr. Adam Lee

Ortega y Ortiz replaced Monsignor Jerome Martinez y Alire as the new rector. Skya announced it was time to write the history of the Altar Society. It was noted that deceased member Miquela Smith had cared for the priest purificators and corporals for 50 years. Deceased member Connie Hernandez donated a large statue of St. Francis. Upon Skya's suggestion, he became the Travelling Francis. Under this structure a member can take him home for a one-month period for personal devotion. He is very popular with the ladies and never without a home! Members vie for this unique spirituality. The Altar Society paid for a bench at Rosario Chapel. Villa Therese Clinic, which the society had supported monthly and yearly, celebrated 75 years.

Skya and Anthony Abbate honored Monsignor Jerome by creating an annual full tuition scholarship worth $70,000 for a student to receive a Master's degree in Acupuncture and Oriental Medicine at Southwest Acupuncture College, called Bind Each Other's Wounds. Former Archbishop Robert F. Sanchez passed away and he was buried under the altar of the Basilica along with many other priests who repose there. Barrack Obama was reelected as president.

The society donated $500 to the Cathedral's trip to Honduras to help the Honduran people in 2013. Bina Rug Co. donated Persian rugs for the sanctuary through the solicitation of member Amelia Hollis. A Continental breakfast was held with St. John's Altar Society to exchange ideas on procedures.

Rev. John C. Wester was installed as Archbishop when Archbishop Sheen retired in 2015. President Skya Abbate suggested that in order to help the many hungry in the local area that members bring two cans of food to each meeting like the Sacred Heart League does. The members responded by bringing a whole bag of groceries to each meeting and have continued this practice to the present.

The Spiritual Development and Writing Club was formed to write this book in 2016 over a two-year period. The Church celebrated the Jubilee Year of Mercy and the Altar Society performed a year of corporal works of mercy. Muhammad Ali died, Donald J. Trump was elected President, and astronaut Neil Armstrong, the first person to step on the moon died. In that act he made "one small step for man, one giant leap for mankind." Between 2006–2016 the society made 610 baptismal garments.

No member was interested in being Vice President, so members alternated monthly in 2017. The decision was made to increase dues from

$15 to $25 starting in 2018. The Writing Club began while hurricanes and violence threatened the United States.

In 2018, the newly instituted Flower Teams continued to be successful in decorating for holy days. The society paid for reupholstering the server benches in the sanctuary. The new banner designed in 2017 by Skya Abbate was being used and members proudly wore their new ribbons and nametags to society and parish events.

Common Activities

Over the years the Altar Society has performed many things consistently. That consistency is a rich mosaic of service that has endured and continues to be meaningful today and for the future. They include but are not limited to the following:

- Making of baptismal garments and lavabos, altar cloths, corporals and purificators
- Support of Villa Therese Catholic Clinic, the clinic adjacent to the church, which "has been bringing healthcare to those in need for 80 years"
- Having Masses said for ill or deceased members of the society along with prayers for those in need
- Giving gifts to clergy and Cathedral staff for Christmas, birthdays, anniversaries, going away events and more
- Purchases of large hangers for clergy vestments
- Purchases of benches and pews, cleaning supplies, holy water font liners, dispensers and other church vessels
- Support of World Youth Day
- Donations to the new sound system
- Support of the music youth program
- Contribution towards the Archbishop's bathroom remodel
- Working harmoniously with parish rectors
- Hostessing and feeding guests at innumerable parish social events
- Meeting consistently for almost 100 years

- Caring for the altar and sanctuaries along with all of the sacred linens
- Participation in the Pastoral Council and the Liturgy Committee
- Caring for the social and spiritual development of its members
- Being both a visible and a hidden presence in the mission of the parish
- Practicing the spirituality of its patron saint, St. Francis of Assisi

Perhaps the broad and poetic insight of President Lyle Quintana Johnson well summarized the years of the St. Francis Altar Society. She writes in her 1977 President's annual report, "Each Altar Society year commences like a jig-saw puzzle, and which piece by piece, incidents large and small, added together, complete the finished picture at the Year's end, fitting into the larger pattern designed by God."

History of the Linens (aka the joys of being a woman!)

- 1948 The Sisters of St. Mary's Convent cared for the linens at $30.00 a month.
- 1950 Fr. Cletus' housekeeper takes over the linens… "And they were beautifully done."
- 1951 Fr. Cletus' housekeeper complains about the amount of linens to wash and iron. The society then decides to use plastic table covers for the side tables to reduce the laundry.
- 1955 A member suggests using the monthly penny collection, typically less than $2.00 a month, to pay for the laundry. It was voted down and wouldn't have helped.
- 1956 The Altar Society takes over the laundry. Members are paid. Mrs. Vigil launders the purificators and Flora Syman does the rest for $30.00. If this works out, laundry bills would be less than $40 a month.
- 1957 Mrs. Ortiz, who does the ironing, requests a raise (but will still do the linens even if she does not receive the raise.) She does receive it and is paid $45.00 a month. In a typical month 213 pieces of linen were sent to her.
- 1959 A lady is paid to do the ironing. She wants to be paid on the first of the month over the 20th.

- 1966 Joseph I. Butler, manager of Interstate Laundry and La Linda Laundry, and husband to Dottie Butler member, does the laundry as a donation. When their son is accepted to Notre Dame, due to this large expenditure, they discontinue the free service.
- 1969 The linens revert to the Altar Society and are then given to La Linda Laundry.
- 1979 Care of the linens continues to be done by the local laundry.
- 1993 Some linens are taken to La Linda Laundry; the members do some.
- 1996 Some linens are missing. It is discovered that Fr. Salvador Aragon is doing the laundry when the women are assigned to it!
- 1998 Fr. Salvador Aragon feels insufficient appreciation is given to Miquela Smith for doing the linens. He notes they are not that dirty. Do they need to be washed as often he asks?
- 2008 President Skya Abbate suggests that the Altar and Sanctuary Committee divides the care of the altar into two branches, cleaning the church and washing and ironing the linens. Under this system each month, two women wash and iron the linens and two to three clean the church weekly.
- Miquela Smith, member, for 50 years cared for the purificators and corporals, which needed special care due to contact with the precious blood.

Figure 19 50th Anniversary Presidents

left to right: Mrs. Robert Ortega, Mrs. Frances Stack, and Mrs. Claude Sena
1971

6

The Presidents

Their Annual Reports, Interviews, and Leadership

"Ours is such a precious and blessed responsibility, caring for the altar and sanctuary of our Eucharistic Lord. What could be sweeter?"

President, Mrs. Mary Reese, 1974

THE ROLE OF THE PRESIDENTS

If flowers are the soul and symbol of the mission of the St. Francis Altar Society, then surely the Presidents were the guardian angels of the group. Through their willingness to serve, to assume responsibility for the work of the society, and to lead the women in service and spirituality, they each made an individual impact on the history of the society, and its ability to meet its mission and to sustain the organization.

The Spiritual Development and Writing Club, to augment the story of the Altar Society told so far, personally interviewed eight Presidents of the St. Francis Altar Society, from 1990 to 2018. They remain members and custodians of the society's history. Theirs is an individual interpretation and retrospective recollection on the St. Francis Altar Society. Firstly, their annual reports are consulted followed by the interviews.

The Annual Reports

The annual reports composed by the Presidents covered a written record of the society's achievements as seen through the eyes of their leaders. Generally, the reports were presented at the first meeting at the start of every New Year. In essence, the contents of most of the reports thanked their officers as well as the society as a whole for the work accomplished in the past year through their service, and highlighted significant events, membership numbers, flower and linen expenses, and hostessing and luncheons. The existing annual reports of the 48 Presidents of the St. Francis Altar Society stem from 1971, the year of the society's 50th Anniversary celebration.

In 1971, then President Mrs. Margaret Bindel on faded onionskin paper in her careful penmanship offered her praise of the women. Her words are timeless and could be said to this very day. Her report reads, "I think it is most appropriate, at this time that you receive a word of grateful appreciation for the good you have accomplished in this society in the spiritual formation of your members, as well as the corporal works of mercy and the caring of the sanctuary and altar. Sincere thanks to each of you for your friendship, work, and interest in this great, blessed, and holy work for the Lord."

Margaret continued in her presidency until 1973. That year she records that Mrs. Jo Romero single handedly tended to 798 purificators, 232 corporals and 31 miscellaneous pieces. Mrs. Rose Fidel did the sewing and mending of surplices, cassocks, albs and more. "Every stitch of her work was for the love of God," Jo relayed. At that time Easter flowers cost $408.54 and Christmas flowers $434.58, a token of what they are today.

Mrs. Mary Reese, President in 1974 wrote, "What does not show up in these reports is all the time and energy expended. Perhaps the recording Angel kept track of this. We didn't. Ours is such a precious and blessed responsibility, caring for the altar and sanctuary of our Eucharistic Lord. What could be sweeter?"

That year, the twice-yearly evening meetings were discontinued because of poor attendance. It was noted that a larger than usual number of members attended the noon luncheon when working members could attend. It was queried, "Perhaps we should consider having noon meetings?"

In 1975, Mrs. Lyle Quintana Johnson wrote in what was to become her characteristic effusiveness, "As we look at where we now stand, we know for a moment the thrill of the little child, who looks at the mark on the wall chart, puts out a trembling little hand as he stands back, then says with pride, 'See how I have grown.' Yes, indeed, during this busy 1975, our members have grown spiritually and in number; and our society has grown materially, for which we thank the dear Lord, realizing that all of these doings were a manifestation of God's power in action—the Holy Spirit working among us."

In 1976, President Quintana wrote about the donation of 12 lovely red satin stoles that were made for the members and worn at the Corporate Communions on the third Sunday of every month. The society was later to learn from a parish priest, Fr. Cyril, that only deacons and priests could wear stoles! Oh well, at least they were lovely!

In 1977, meetings began to be held at the Inn of the Governors, a local hotel, as there were too many members to meet in the members' homes. The first Altar Society banner was also made and used until 2017 when President Skya Abbate designed a new one in anticipation of the one-hundred-year anniversary of the society in 2021. Dues were raised from $6 to $10.

President Mrs. Geraldine Murphy in 1978 noted a fact that remains true to today. She said,"I write this easily but I would like to emphasize that the parish could not do without the hundreds of hours of work done by this group."She also offers advice for the future in connection with the experience referring to the first red satin Altar Society banner. "The next time, any of the members should offer to make something of that nature, that their offer should be accepted as the work would be a labor of love and as nearly perfect as humanly possible."

In 1979, under President Frances Martinez, there were 148 members with 25–30 attending the monthly meetings, much like it is now with meeting attendance, despite the number of members. She thanked Lyle Johnson for her interesting meditations that were provided for each meeting. Frances reminded the ladies that the personal sanctification of the women was the primary purpose of the society, and secondarily the care of the altars and sanctuaries, but that both were important.

Muriel Gondeck was the President in 1980 and 1981. In 1981, Mass was said for the prisoners who died during the riots at the Santa Fe Penitentiary, an event that rocked the Santa Fe community. In her handwritten scroll on Altar Society stationery she writes that at this point Corporate Communions were not well attended. In her second year, Rev. Fr. Reynaldo Rivera of the Cathedral was shockingly murdered on a house call. The society received the Dove Award for the highest attendance at the Santa Fe Church Women United. With the buffer that they purchased for $54.00 the women noted that they struggled to keep the altar railing "nice and shiny! Next President Emilia Sedillo joyfully expounded, "It keeps us nice and trim."

In 1983, under Emilia Sedillo, membership was at 153 members and from 25 to 35 members attended the monthly meetings. She boasted, "Fresh flowers adorned our altar every day of the year." "A million thanks were given to Lyle Johnson who continued to write her monthly meditations for the meetings." Helen Wheeler and her husband were thanked for delivering 750 gifts donated by the Altar Society members to patients of the New Mexico State Hospital, a facility for the mentally impaired, in Las Vegas, New Mexico.

In 1984, Fr. Crispin asked the members to make baptismal robes for the babies who received baptism at the Cathedral and this practice has continued for 34 years, since then to the present. A membership drive brought in 30 new members after an announcement was made in the parish bulletin for two weeks and was followed by a coffee and donut social.

At this point, the altar railing, once thought polished to perfection by the new buffer, apparently was scratching it. Also, the priests complained that it was making noise during confession, so it was back to polishing the rail by hand! Beautifully wrapped gifts were showered upon the New Mexico State Hospital. The hospital thanked the women and commented that the nightgowns and other items were beautiful but it would be best if they were not wrapped so that so that they could be appropriately distributed.

In 1986, Lucille c'de Baca was President. The Centennial celebration of the Cathedral was held. Then mayor, Louis R. Montano, made an official city proclamation that February 16, 1986 was the "65th Birthday of the Santa Fe Altar Society Day." On the framed proclamation he bestowed upon the society he asked the members "to enjoy and set aside this day for all your unselfish time and dedication."

From 1987 to 1988 Rosina LaBadie served as President. As expected, there was a mound of Christmas presents for the New Mexico State Hospital. It was a hard year for the Altar Society with a shortage of help due to illness and other unforeseen reasons. Rosina eloquently observed,

> These weekly cleanings, as well as the special cleanings for Easter, Fiestas and Christmas should not be regarded as chores or drudgeries. It is the reason for our being—the purpose of our society. Cleaning in the house of God should be an act of love—indeed a privilege. How many people have the opportunity to dust the table of God? Touch the purificator that wipes the chalice, which contained the body and blood of Christ? The lavabo towels, which dry the fingers, which have touched the body and blood of Christ? These acts of love do not escape the eyes and heart of God. And remember, He cannot be outdone in love or generosity.

The making of the little baptismal robes continued, and 148 robes were cut in record time. Ana Mae Vigil moaned of the blisters to show for it in 1975! A combined luncheon with the Sacred Heart League for deceased Monsignor Barcello was held. The society assessed that it was a pleasure working with the members of the Sacred Heart League. Helen Wheeler, 1989 President, and her husband made"the leisurely drive to Las Vegas with the gifts for the New Mexico State Hospital." Sincere thanks were given by the hospital to the Altar Society for their thoughtfulness and generosity. Beloved Fr. Austin died on December 21 to spend a Christmas in heaven! There was no reason for sadness.

In 1989, the Pastoral Council was formed to guide the parish in its overall mission, and the Altar Society like other parish ministries, was part of that. Gifts to the hospital continued.

Amelia Hollis was the President in 1990. She noted that the society was back in the catering business, referring to all of the cooking and serving functions the society was called upon to do.

In 1991, Pat Gonzales presided. The Dove Award was presented to the Altar Society for their high representation at Church Women United. A Leprosy Pig, named Francsco, was used to collect money for the American Leprosy Society. Clothes were collected for St. Michael's Arizona Mission, and gifts continued to amass for New Mexico State Hospital and brought to them for Christmas by Pat Gonzales' brother. Pat concluded, "Our active members are a small group, but we have a small army behind us that support and help us when called upon."

In 2004, President Mary Louise Giron summarized the work of the group after her service. "We did our purpose. We need to address our need to grow in holiness." The next nominated President, Skya Abbate, pondered this insight for future action.

In 2005, Skya Abbate was elected President and has held that position for 14 years. Even though the norm had been one to two years its allowance was done through a waiver in the By-Laws that was part of the amended Constitution and the wisdom of the members. Notable achievements of the society included utilization of media such as the parish bulletin for items of interest, computerization of minutes, agendas, and mailing lists, the implementation of the annual retreats, and the writing of this book. One of the things she is most humbled by is the monthly collection of food for the St. Vincent de Paul store, as hunger is an especial concern of the women, that she suggested. She is also happy that the circulation of a statue of St. Francis to individual members' homes was viewed as spirituality. The annual retreats, at which Skya has been the retreat leader and only presenter for ten years has been a highlight and a fulfillment of that call to holiness that Mary Louise invited the members to. She notes retrospectively that going forward, the annual reports should be continued for the history of the Altar Society, its members, and parishioners, to celebrate and document achievements and revitalize the society.

The Interviews

To augment the annual reports and minutes of the Altar Society, members of the Spiritual Development and Writing Club conducted interviews with the eight living Presidents. The framing of their presidencies is captured in those narratives. The Presidents highlight what they think is important to know about the Altar Society.

Amelia Hollis, 1990

Amelia Hollis became President in 1990. To date she has been a member of the Altar Society for over forty years. During her time as President, the Seder Meal (Passover) was introduced and served in Crispin Hall and the St. Francis School gym. Later the *Semana Santa* meal during Holy Week was introduced by longstanding member Carmen Dofflemeyer and hosted and served by the Altar Society. The food consisted of meatless dishes and a variety of delicious entrees and desserts brought in by the parishioners and was well attended as a communal celebration prior to the *Triduum*.

Yearly, the Altar Society was in charge of setting up an altar outside of the Cathedral during the Corpus Christi processions as a public testimony of faith outside of church auspices. On Thanksgiving and Christmas holidays baskets of food were prepared and distributed by the Altar Society to families in need. The Altar Society always fixed a table in the plaza for the blessing of the palms on Palm Sunday. Birthday, get well, and sympathy cards were sent to members and their families.

The Altar Society hosted many fundraiser receptions such as the Silver Teas at the Governor's Mansion. During her presidency, a reception of tamales and *biscochitos* on Our Lady of Guadalupe feast day began and lasted a number of years. Amelia was Pastoral Council President for a several years and co-chair of the 400th Anniversary of the Cathedral.

Patricia Gonzales, 1991–1992

Pat joined the St. Francis Altar Society in 1984, 34 years ago! Pat recalls that she enjoyed the years when the Silver Tea fundraiser was held in the Governor's Mansion. She felt invitations to the mansion were politically motivated and so sometimes the society was not able to use that venue for the fundraising activities of the group.

One of her favorite activities in the society was embroidering baptismal garments. She shared a humorous story about going camping, which she did often, and inviting members who also liked embroidering. She would give each of them five garments to embroider and she would come home with twenty-five garments, which were completed during their camping trip, accompanied by much talk and laughter. Some women had to embroider more than five garments because she said some of the ladies were very slow. Sounds like fun!

Pat remembers cleaning the pews in the church for Easter and Christmas, in addition to the normal areas of the sacristies, sanctuary, and confessionals. The ladies would also collect money for flowers during Masses for those special feast days. She mentioned that the Blessed Sacrament Chapel was off limits for cleaning as Miquela Smith, one of the Altar Society members, was solely in charge of everything to do with the Chapel. Another activity she recalls was the collection of clothes for the needy in Arizona. Candy Johnson and Lucille c' de Baca and others packed their car and delivered the clothes yearly to the nearby state.

She vividly recounts going with a friend to a warehouse market in town, filling a tiny Volkswagen vehicle with all the items needed for making many trays of finger sandwiches for the various receptions held at the

Cathedral. She enjoyed the friendships made during these activities and missed the Franciscans when they left because of declining vocations. She warmly remembers Fr. Crispin.

Mary Jane Martinez, 1995–1996

First of all, I must say that since I served as President from 1995 to 1996 and most of 1993 to 1994 due to our President's illness with multiple sclerosis, I don't recall very many details during those years. However, I do have vivid memories of holding our annual Silver Teas at the Governor's Mansion. Those were memorable events.

Most of what I mention here are the trials that occurred during my 30 years from 1987 to 2017 as member of the Altar Society. They include: not having a Spiritual Director, losing the privilege of purchasing flowers, and receiving half of the money collection for sanctuary needs that is now split with the administration of the parish.

I believe a new President should have thorough communications with the Spiritual Director (if we have one) as well as the Altar Society members. Most members have influenced me since they are always willing to do whatever needs to be done whether it is cleaning, ironing, serving at receptions, volunteering at homeless shelters or their donations to many charities.

Mercedes Roybal, 1997–1998

Elementary school teacher Mercedes Roybal recalls the many functions and duties that an Altar Society President bore. For her some of the highlights were the many receptions that she oversaw such as the ordinations of priests, deacons, and other social events. At that time there was no money for caterers and the Altar Society did it all—organizing, purchasing ingredients, serving and hostessing.

In 1998, the society was invited to be part of the Liturgy Committee. The letter of invitation to the Liturgy Committee acknowledged that the Altar Society was an integral part of parish liturgies and they would welcome our input and the gift of talents that the Altar Society shares with the parish. Amelia Hollis was the representative to the committee and the liaison to the Altar Society. The society noted that the committee's work deserves praise for the strategically placed flower arrangements that enhanced the overall view of the sanctuary.

Leonor Anaya Mead, 1999–2000

During her term as President, Leonor recounts, the Franciscan priests left the parish and were replaced by secular priests. While their departure was bittersweet, a new beginning flourished under Father Jerome Martinez y Alire as the new rector. He was certainly a ray of sunshine. Not only were there many badly needed repairs to the Cathedral but much needed camaraderie amongst the parishioners that he attended to. We learned that altar cloths, vestments, flowers and our work at the altar should be in Father Jerome's words, "of Cathedral quality" and that is what it has become. The Altar Society Silver Tea, which was held every summer, ended and the parish-wide picnics were introduced so fundraising for the society ended. Altar Society members also cooked and served at many receptions hosted by the Cathedral. Today caterers supply most of the food.

In 2000, under Leonor, the society made an amendment to Article IV of the Constitution and By-Laws to change the meeting dates from the third Monday to the third Wednesday of the month as it currently is to accommodate Msgr. Jerome's schedule.

Tessie Anchondo, 2001–2002

Tessie Anchondo joined the St. Francis Altar Society in 1996. She was the Secretary from 1997 to 1998, Vice President from 1999 to 2000, and President from 2001 to 2002. As President she presided over forty active members. She learned the roles of the different positions from previous officers and never felt alone. All members were very cooperative and well informed on what to do. She presided as Vice President when the Franciscan priests were at the Cathedral.

Sometimes two priests would attend the Altar Society meetings. One of the things she enjoyed most was the Silver Tea at the Governor's Mansion. A lot of work went into them because they were fundraisers. She also enjoyed decorating the church for different feast days and holidays. She learned flower arranging from Chris Carrey, an artist and parishioner from *Santa Maria de La Paz* parish, who taught the society how to arrange the flowers in large vases, for the church. "They looked so professional," she adds.

Tessie is involved in many church ministries; for example, she is Nocturnal Adoration President and Charter member of Treasures of Wisdom senior ministry where she held all offices. She enjoys fellowship in working with all members of the Altar Society and with her other ministries.

Mary Louise Giron, 2003–2004

Mary Louise Giron has been an active member of the St. Francis Altar Society for over twenty years. From 1997 to 1998, she served as a volunteer school nurse at the St. Francis School and was active in the Boy Scout movement. She then joined the Altar Society to serve her church community. She became Secretary, Vice President, and then President and Member of the Liturgy Committee.

During her term as President Mary Louise recalls, "I was inspired by the immense ideas that Monsignor Jerome Martinez y Alire brought to the Church. He was progressive and a great spiritual leader. We worked to help Monsignor replace artificial décor with fresh flowers, terra cotta vases, and greenery which made our altars beautiful beyond words." Instead of fundraisers Monsignor introduced the idea of an Altar Society Collection Envelope for all parishioners to contribute towards the costs of sanctuary needs, flowers, and other things. "The Constitution was also updated to include any person, that is, also men. Due to unforeseen problems with men we remain a ladies' organization." She concludes,"Thank you for the opportunity to serve as an officer of this great organization."

Skya Abbate, 2005–2018

As the most long-standing President of the Altar Society, 14 years as opposed to one or two, and the author of this book, Skya's perspective on the Altar Society is broad and deep. She hopes that this book will serve as a model for future Presidents and members.

Skya wrote her Masters degree thesis in 2012 called *My Ministry Understanding and Decisions as President of the St. Francis Altar Society—Oasis of Grace in the Desert*[1] with Loyola University, New Orleans, where she

1. Abbate, *My Ministry.*

gained one of her three Masters degrees, this one in Pastoral Studies and Christian Spirituality. Therein she analyzed the society from the framework of how the society meets the definition of ministry within the Catholic faith tradition.

She reflects that her personal goals have always aimed at genuinely honoring the gifts each member possesses and recognizes that she heads up a people of imagination with a sense of ownership and deep involvement in the church. Her strong sense of Catholic history and spirituality from grammar school through to the doctoral level, has prompted her to continue to advocate our service to the altar of the world through charitable giving and personal community involvement in an economically poor state and a poor world, with all of its concomitant problems, just like the members have as the 100 year anniversary approaches.

Skya claims her theology of ministry shapes her leadership style. She strives to forge collegial friendships under what she hopes is collaborative leadership. She tries to facilitate and to bring the members to conclusions through active listening, and promote loving conversations open to transformation. She likes to invite, encourage, and connect ideas, and empower the members and make them feel good about themselves and their ministry. This is accomplished by taking the time to divulge the mental maps of members and establishing a safe, sensitive, and trustful atmosphere for discussion, inquiry, and reflection, where "risks for kingdom of God are taken" —part of the parish's mission statement, which proves to be an easy venture in the company of holy women! And she adds, "I do like to lead! This ministerial outlook has been the secret to the fulfillment of the many tasks of the society, has fostered and sustained membership, and has engendered artistic, personal, cultural and spiritual transformation.

Skya writes in her thesis, "My leadership praxis of imagination, integrity, and inclusivity is my labor of love served at the altar of my faith. To bring the members into the post-Vatican II world of vital participation by the laity exhilarates me. My ministerial outlook has transformed my normal business style leadership to servant, reduced my pride to humility, and my attachment to non-attachment—appropriate attitudes in service to the church. I am a symbolic leader in imitation of Christ, in my mind what I call real presence, and I strive to use this power reflectively. I will always be a member of the St. Francis Altar Society."

Presidents 1921–2018

In grateful appreciation and admiration of the Presidents (known) of the St. Francis Altar Society who led the group towards its 100 years of service. May God bless your service to the altar and your response to its call in the world. Who will lead us into to the future? It could be you!

Table 1.The Presidents

1	Mrs. May Murphy	1921–1923
2	Mrs. Mary Hurley	1923–1926
3	Mrs. Ann Davies	1937
4	Mrs. Josephine Harkins	1938
5	Mrs. John McConvery	1939
6	Mrs. Myrtle Read	1940
7	Miss Anita Bergere	1941
8	Mrs. C.D. Van Hecke	1942
9	Mrs. Dan T. Kelly, Sr.	1943
10	Mrs. Wolcott Russell	1945
11	Mrs. Frank Ortiz y Davis	1946
12	Mrs. Ruth B. Jones	1947
13	Mrs. R. P. Sweeney	1948
14	Mrs. John Hopson	1949–1950
15	Mrs. Joseph Moya	1951
16	Mary Chapman	1952
17	Mrs. Thomas B. Walsh	1953
18	Mrs. Howell Earnest	1954
19	Ruth McIntyre	1955
20	Mrs. Frank McCulloch and Mrs. Manual (Jean) Lujan	both
21	Mrs. Edmund Di Lorenzo	1956
22	Mrs. Phillip (Esther B.) Sanchez	1957–1958
23	Mrs. Dorothy Miller	1959
24	Anna McCullough	1960
25	Mrs. Francis (Katy) Stack	1961–1962
26	Mrs. Roberto Ortega	1963–1964
27	Mrs. Claude Sena	1965–1966

28	Mrs. Joseph Butler	1966–1967
29	Mrs. Floyd (Elsie) Haake	1967–1970
30	Margaret Bindel	1971–1972
31	Mary Reese	1973–1974
32	Lyle Q. Johnson	1975–1977
33	Geraldine Murphy	1978
34	Frances Martinez	1978–1980
35	Muriel Gondeck	1981–1982
36	Emelia Sedillo	1983–1984
37	Lucille c'de Baca	1986
38	Rosina LaBadie	1987
39	Helen Wheeler	1988–1989
40	Amelia Hollis	1990
41	Patricia Gonzales	1991–1992
42	Becky Archuleta	1993–1994
43	Mary Jane Martinez	1995–1996
44	Mercedes Roybal	1997–1988
45	Leonor Mead	1999–2000
46	Tessie Anchondo	2001–2002
47	Mary Louise Giron	2003–2004
48	Skya Abbate	2005–2018

Figure 20 Garden Party

At the home of Postmaster and Mrs. Edward Berardinelli
Mrs. Floyd Haake, Mrs. Katherine Fladung, and Mrs. Thomas Walsh
1956

7

The Silver Teas

Traditions of Hospitality, 1927–1995

"Our table was exquisite."

Pat Gonzales, Altar Society President, 1991

THE SILVER TEAS

If scrapbooks hold special memories and attest to what we want to remember, then the immensely popular Silver Teas held by the St. Francis Altar Society were special collective memories documented in an entire album from 1956 to 1970. Annually, they were held in the summer and were the society's largest fundraiser and the most outstanding event of the year. The money raised by donations to the Silver Teas was used to furnish the Cathedral with needed items to care for the altars, sanctuary, and church as well as to purchase the floral arrangements for the liturgical year. The combined efforts of the society met the two major functions of the mission statement, that is, to care for the altar and sanctuary, and to promote parish and member sociability.

The New Mexican, the local Santa Fe newspaper, reports the following story.

> According to the historians of the Altar Society the first Silver Tea was organized in 1927 by Amalia Sena Sanchez who was the Fiesta Queen that year along with other 'pioneer social leaders,' Anita Grant, Clara Sweeney, Anita Bergere and Mary Gormley. It was *de rigueur* in the early days to accessorize the tea finery with Chinese silk, Philippine lace mantillas, or hats and gloves. Members recall sashaying with such paraphernalia through some of Santa Fe's finest showplaces where the teas were held such as the stately pink colored Bergere home on Grant Avenue, the Roybal residence at Paseo de Peralta and Galisteo, the Greer Mansion on Paseo de Peralta, and the Callecita residence of Della Montoya and U.S. Senator Manuel Montoya.[1]

Records attest that the Silver Teas were very well organized. Every member took part in carrying out the necessary duties. Those jobs were dispersed amongst 14 or more committees! For instance, for the 1989 Silver Tea there were the following committees: Publicity, Invitations, Receiving Line, Member Nametags, Guest Book, Silver Bowl, Entertainment, Pouring Hostesses, Table Appointments, Hostesses, Food Committee, Telephone Committee, Kitchen, Tea Preparers, and Tray Captains.

Personal invitations were mailed to the Cathedral parishioners as well as members of the public and other faiths. Radio coverage and announcements in the parish bulletin augmented the personal invitations. The teas also were well publicized in advance in the *Que Pasa* section of the local newspaper, *The New Mexican,* and the newspaper wrote many articles about them after the event. Voluminous surviving photos from 1971 to 1989 come from that newspaper. They depict the Altar Society members, the Governor's wives, and the public elegantly dressed and having fun in the spacious homes, enclosed portals, large terraces, sheltered patios and summer gardens of the hostesses' residences. The Berardinelli gardens were always beautiful with their shrubs, trees, annuals and perennials, and offered soft contrast to the distant mountains. At the same time, nature was at her summer zenith. Conspiracies of crickets scratched their wings in wonder when the double winged dragonfly dipped its diaphanous wings reverently into a cool granite birdbath. One bird sipped meditatively from the birdbath where a red African daisy floated in reverie of its native land. Another bird jumped in and splashed with delight as all the guests watched in astonishment.

1. McCarty, *The Santa Fe New Mexican.*

In 1956, *The New Mexican* noted that the society was open to all English-speaking women in the parish. They also commented on the community support of the Altar Society to the Milk Depot. The Milk Depot was an effort primarily financed by the Santa Fe Council of Catholic Women and dispensed by the Santa Fe Women's Club and Library Association. The Altar Society members brought one large can of milk to every meeting for those less fortunate to obtain milk for their infants and very young children.

In August 1960 at the Silver Tea, an approaching rainstorm combined with notorious Santa Fe dust created a dramatic and vivid background at the home of Mrs. Antonio Fernandez high on a hill with sweeping views of the Sandia, *Sangre de Cristo*, and Jemez Mountains. The simmering thunder of the approaching afternoon monsoon stirred the sleeping birds from the trees, and they called out to each other to take other shelter in a prearranged place beneath the gathering grey clouds as the ladies retreated to the portals for their cover.

In her 1981 Silver Tea Report, Chairwoman Mary Reese wrote, "Well, the Tea is over for another year—it was a lot of work—but wasn't it fun?" On July 21,1982, at the home of Dr. and Mrs. Luis J. Bernardez we read,"As usual Bobbi Gallegos was able to easily keep two punch bowls replenished with her refreshing fruit punch. Everyone was ready for another cool drink this warm afternoon."

Lace table clothes and sparkling pieces of silver and crystal loaned to the society for the long tea tables made an elegant presentation. An heirloom silver bowl, often surrounded by seasonal flowers, was used to collect donations for the event, and coordinated with flaming red gladiolas and white baby's breath or cool shades of home grown blue flower centerpieces. While the ladies, nimble as butterflies danced throughout the house at their tasks, their natural counterparts made a fast dash for the pink lemonade and emerged with smiles as broad as their bedazzling wings.

At their inception in 1927, the teas were first held in the private homes of the members in July when access to the beauty of outdoor gardens was available. In 1953, one of the first Silver Teas recorded in the scrapbook was held at the residence of Governor John F. Sims (1955–1957). Other Governors hostessing the Silver Teas were U.S. Senator and Mrs. Joseph Montoya, Governor Bruce King (1971–1975), Governor Jerry Apodaca (1975–1979), and Governor Gary Carrruthers (1987–1991). The last Silver Tea was held in 1995 at the residence of Governor Gary Johnson (1995–2003). During the Governor Johnson administration, the teas ended at the venue of the

Governor's residence because the Altar Society was raising and collecting money and the Governor deemed this politically incorrect. After that, the Silver Teas were held at the Cathedral gardens or in Father Crispin Hall.

There were very specific rules for using the Governors' residences that included the time frame for the event, parking, and the clean up crew but highlights at the Silver Teas were always delicious food as well as great entertainment. The members made dainty refreshments such as sandwiches, brownies, cupcakes, nut breads, cookies, *pastelito*s and *biscochitos*. The society provided beautiful floral arrangements for the event. The residence offered coffee and tea, and the State police security force ensured safety. Cathedral Choir Director, Melisendro Ortiz, many times proffered music accompanied by the choir. There were other musicians and dance groups that consisted of youngsters, and a senior dance group called *Los Coloniales*. The largest attendance at the 1987 Silver Tea was 400 people at the home of Mrs. Gary Carruthers, wife of the Governor, a charming first lady who stood in line for 2 hours to welcome guests. She noted this was the largest number of people the mansion had ever hosted for any event!

Ticket holders had a chance to win a special item at the teas. In 1975 a beautiful silver and turquoise necklace was the prize. Silver bowl contributions, in which the participants donated money for the fundraiser, typically made $300—$900 net profit after expenses. Donations could also be mailed to the Altar Society.

The chapters on the Years and the Presidents offer further testament to the enjoyment that the members took in these undertakings. After a long history the lovely Silver Teas came to an end. Fundraising to meet the needs of the society for the care of the altars and sanctuaries, flower purchasing and their other works in social justice in supporting the community was rather propitiously achieved by the newly instituted annual Altar Society Collection Envelope to supplement the Christmas and Easter flower envelopes used for flower purchasing. In this golden time, the Silver Teas more than met their financial goals and offered rich opportunities for building collegiality amongst the membership and presence in the parish and the community.

Reflection by Lyle Quintana Johnson of the Flower Committee for the Silver Tea July 9, 1980 at the Governor's Residence

An abundance of lovely summer flowers surrounded the carved wooden stature of St. Francis with his birds, which made up the centerpiece on the long tea table. The statute came from the little old fishing village of Zihuataneo, on the blue Pacific, which is south of the border far down Mexico way in the tropics. The same colorful flowers were used in the mound around the wooden stature of St. Francis carved by Efran Martinez of Santa Fe, which was on the side table, and these same flowers also encircled the miniature Ben Ortega St. Francis statue that was placed at the silver bowl. These lovely floral arrangements were the creation of The Flower Nook and my donation to the tea. Afterwards Elsie Haake took the flowers to the Granada Nursing Home, some for our beloved member Valerie Gough, who has been there the last few months, and the rest for the enjoyment of all the other patients residing there.

Now a short flower meditation based on Brother Brian's talk at our June meeting during which he refers to the flowers in the bowl on the table, which incidentally were beautiful roses. "All the flowers of all the tomorrows are seeds of today and seldom do we realize that the glory and the power of Him who made the universe lie hidden in a flower."

Figure 21 The Presidents: Working for Social Justice

Left to right: Leonor A. Mead, Patricia Gonzales, Mary Louise Giron, Skya Abbate, Amelia Hollis, and Tessie Anchondo

CYCLE OF LIFE

Dearest Lord,
Thank you for the gift of life
Bestowed at Conception
Enfleshed at Birth
Magnified at Baptism
Cleansed through Reconciliation
Nourished by the Eucharist
Inspired at Confirmation
Multiplied by Holy Matrimony
Consecrated in Holy Orders
Anointed in the Sacrament of the Sick.
For those who suffer
Enslaved in poverty
Incarcerated by crime
Injured in human trafficking
Ignored in abortion
Restricted in immigration
We pray through your mercy
Bless them
Sanctify them
Give them a life of dignity
For either in sacramental participation or secularism
We all partake of your human and divine essence
So too, we are all made to return to you
Our origin and destiny. Amen
By Skya Abbate

8

Peace and Social Justice

Serving the Altar of the World

"FRANCIS, GO REPAIR MY HOUSE. YOU SEE IT IS ALL FALLING DOWN."

Voice from the crucifix to Francis

A SURPRISE ASSOCIATION?

WHETHER IN CONSCIOUS IMITATION of their patron, St. Francis of Assisi, the natural inclination of the human heart, or the promptings the Roman Catholic Church, since its very inception through to the present day, the St. Francis Altar Society has been an advocate of peace and social justice in their parish and throughout the world. They have honored the church's position on the preferential treatment of the poor and special concern for the oppressed. Most of their work in peace and social justice has been an operating principle of the group stemming from its inception in 1921 and is a fact not well known by the parish or even the society. Hence, the perspective provided by history illumines this surprising ideological, spiritual, and practical thread.

In what appears to be the 1977 Constitution, that document in Article III, Section 7 reads, "The Community Action Committee shall promote

Christian action, both social and economic in the community. They shall be responsible for the courtesies extended to members in illness or sorrow, and shall especially endeavor to assist the aged." Section 8 enlarges that service beyond the parish to read, "The World Responsibility Committee shall assist the pastor with the clothing and fund drives of the Bishop's Relief and any other program undertaken by the church toward world unity and understanding."

Although these particular committees phased out during the society's history this outreach became subsumed under the overall work of the society. The actual acts of charity, peace, and social justice throughout the long history of the society are too many to recount although many are documented in the minutes. The writing committee of this book highlighted some of the more notable ones in the chapters on the Years and the Presidents. Other works derived from the study of the historical documents deserve special attention. Additionally, at times, honors, awards, and recognition were bestowed upon the society.

On June 20, 1960, the *Las Damas* (the women) de Santa Fe Charter, celebrating their 350th anniversary, presented the society with a certificate for participating in wearing originals or copies of costumes of "olden days," defined as predating 1900. The woman had to wear the clothes one day a week for eight weeks prior to the anniversary. That must have been an interesting sight to see the women in their costumes honor those ancestors who make up the history of Santa Fe!

Support for national and international wars and disasters had long been a hallmark of the society. Food, money, and clothing collections during World War I (1914–1918) through to America's involvement with the Vietnam War are noted. One rather poignant letter was written to the Altar Society, what I call the "Christmas Day Letter," from the Sargent of the 23rd Infantry division. This letter is particularly moving retrospectively considering the unpopularity of the Vietnam War at the time for Americans. The Altar Society cared for these unknown men who suffered rejection, isolation, and ostracism at that time and on this special holiday. It speaks for itself of the society's support of the Western Americal Division in 1970.

The Dove Award was given out to celebrate the World Day of Prayer in 1982 to the Altar Society for their high representation at Church Women United. In 1983 the society participated in constructing a segment of a ribbon, one of many thousands of pieces made throughout Santa Fe, New Mexico and the nation that would form a mile-long ribbon. On the 40th anniversary of the bombing of Hiroshima and Nagasaki the ribbon was draped around the Pentagon in Washington, D.C. as a statement that the United States should strive for peace. Resident artist of the Altar Society, Clorinda Garcia, designed and painted the ribbon with symbols of what Catholics said they would most miss in the event of a nuclear war. The design depicted a chalice and a host, and a church and a family. It seems like they captured those realities very well!The words attributed to St. Francis,

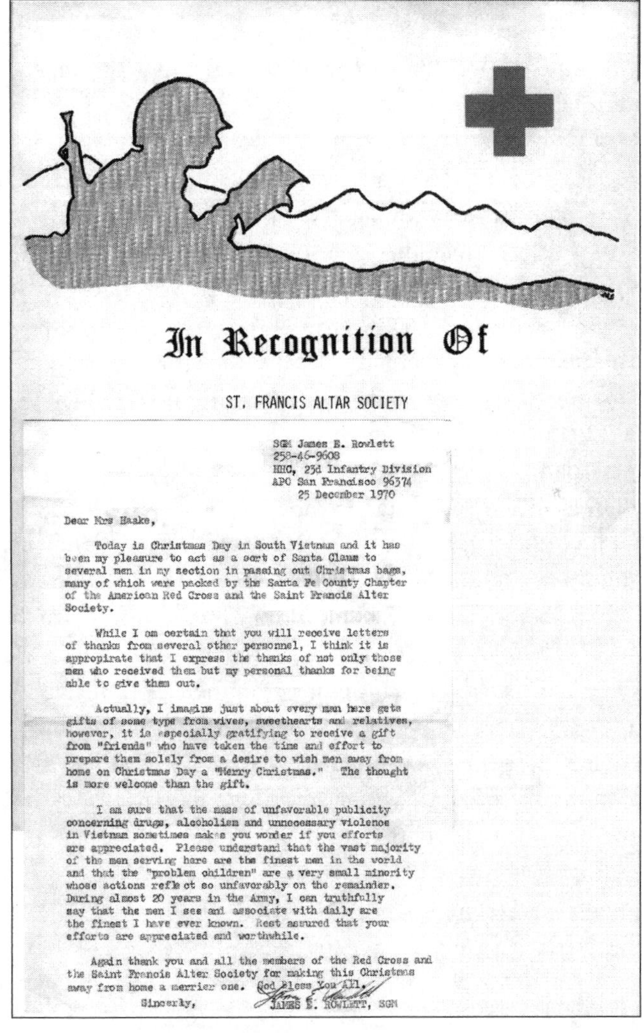

In Recognition Of

ST. FRANCIS ALTAR SOCIETY

SGM James E. Rowlett
258-46-9608
HHC, 23d Infantry Division
APO San Francisco 96374
25 December 1970

Dear Mrs Haake,

Today is Christmas Day in South Vietnam and it has been my pleasure to act as a sort of Santa Claus to several men in my section in passing out Christmas bags, many of which were packed by the Santa Fe County Chapter of the American Red Cross and the Saint Francis Alter Society.

While I am certain that you will receive letters of thanks from several other personnel, I think it is appropirate that I express the thanks of not only those men who received them but my personal thanks for being able to give them out.

Actually, I imagine just about every man here gets gifts of some type from wives, sweethearts and relatives, however, it is especially gratifying to receive a gift from "friends" who have taken the time and effort to prepare them solely from a desire to wish men away from home on Christmas Day a "Merry Christmas." The thought is more welcome than the gift.

I am sure that the mass of unfavorable publicity concerning drugs, alcoholism and unnecessary violence in Vietnam sometimes makes you wonder if you efforts are appreciated. Please understand that the vast majority of the men serving here are the finest men in the world and that the "problem children" are a very small minority whose actions reflect so unfavorably on the remainder. During almost 20 years in the Army, I can truthfully say that the men I see and associate with daily are the finest I have ever known. Rest assured that your efforts are appreciated and worthwhile.

Again thank you and all the members of the Red Cross and the Saint Francis Alter Society for making this Christmas away from home a merrier one. God Bless You All.

Sincerly,

JAMES E. ROWLETT, SGM

Figure 22 The Christmas Day Letter

"Lord make us a channel of your peace," were also emblazoned on the ribbon segment. Today the entire ribbon is found in the permanent exhibition at the Peace Museum in Chicago.

Locally, on its 65th birthday, the mayor declared February 16, 1986, the St. Francis Altar Society Day. He encouraged the members to rest and to cherish this day. In 1988, cards were sent to disabled veterans. The Leprosy Pig, named Francisco, was used to collect money for the American Leprosy Society in 1991. Francis would have liked that since one of his ways to following in the footsteps of Christ was to literally clothe and embrace the lepers of his time, an appalling act to those who could not understand the radical love of Christ.

In May 2010 a Certificate of Appreciation for their "outstanding spirit of volunteerism serving the homeless men, women, and children of Santa Fe at the Interfaith Shelter with dignity and respectful hospitality" was presented to the society. Since then the society has participated with several parish ministries and other denominations in Santa Fe that provide a minimum of one meal a year to 100–250 people at a time to the homeless at the shelter. The members have opted to spend their own money augmented by some membership money totaling several hundred dollars per year to provide a nutritious, evening winter meal. Typically the menu consists of fresh green salad, a meat entrée such as chicken, and a carbohydrate like baked potatoes, beans, or pasta. Members serve the food and check the homeless into the shelter for the night. The members enjoy this service and find it a humbling and spiritual experience to meet and feed the homeless.

The Villa Theresa Catholic Clinic located on the grounds of the Cathedral property offer free dental and medical care to the poor. Historically, the Altar Society has been a staunch supporter of their work through monthly donations, participation in raffles, or other events sponsored by the clinic.

Prisoners were always a population that the Altar Society served. From providing them with Catholic reading materials, to other corporal works of mercy such as letters on a regular basis, to money to purchase small comfort items from the prison canteens, the Altar Society offered nonjudgmental and loving support to these brethren.

As referred to in the Years and the Presidents chapters, the New Mexico State Hospital in Las Vegas, New Mexico was the recipient of continued, dedicated, and voluntary service to the patients with a trove of Christmas gifts delivered to them by the society's members. Gifts were given at least from 1984 to1991. In January 1983, the society was presented with a certificate of appreciation for their continued dedication and voluntary service to the patients of the hospital. It is hard to say who enjoyed this seasonal sharing more!

Later, almost $1000 was raised on the spot at a meeting in 2011 to aid those affected by the Japanese tsunami and nuclear aftermath, representing a spontaneous outpouring of global humanitarian concern. While times have changed, this is a lot of money from a small group of women yet it parallels the collection of spare pennies taken at the meetings to help in world war efforts.

Over the years many Altar Society members received the St. Francis Award, a special honor given yearly to a single member or a couple from every parish in the archdiocese for service to their parish in multiple ministries. They have included the following Altar Society members and spouses.

- Deacon Juan and Mary Jane Martinez 2003
- Miquela Smith 2004
- Frank and Carmen Dofflemeyer 2005
- Angie Kollasch 2012
- Dolores Garcia 2013
- Hermine and Gerald Quintana 2015

In 2017, in anticipation of the 100th anniversary of the society in 2021, President Skya Abbate designed the new St. Francis Altar Society banner to now depict Francis as the Patron Saint of Ecology. It features a green globe fashioned in swatches of textured silk with the words, "God so loved the world," taken from John 3:16. The background of the world is a cream colored canvas befitting the simplicity of Francis. The intent of this banner, now in the newly adopted colors of the St. Francis Altar Society of brown, white, and green, was to extend our service of the altar from the local parish to the larger matrix of human and incarnational life. Interestingly, in 1979 President Lyle Quintana Johnson foreshadowed this thought. She wrote in her October meditation, "Certainly his attitude towards creatures and creation is sorely needed today lest our natural resources disappear from the environment. Methinks that St. Francis would be a happy choice for the Patron Saint of Ecology." We agree as our society celebrates our sacred planet with this unpretentious yet regal banner.

Just this year, the small Peace and Social Justice Committee at the Basilica was no longer functional as it slowly devolved over the last ten years.

It is a harbinger of a failed ministry due to the lack of leadership, membership, and long range-plans. While the articulated mission of the St. Francis Altar Society may never change, as maintained in this chapter, peace and social justice have animated the society and have been its response like Francis' to repair God's church. The Altar Society has the unique position and foundation to assume upon our humble mantle a response to the voice of Jesus to rebuild a social and ecclesial order rooted in the love of Christ for our parish and world.

Figure 23 The 2018 retreat

9

Prayers, Spiritualties, and Annual Retreats

Regrouping, Rethinking, and Rededication

"KEEP WATCH OVER YOUR MANNER OF LIFE, DEAR PEOPLE, AND MAKE SURE THAT YOU ARE INDEED THE LORD'S LABORERS. EACH PERSON SHOULD TAKE INTO ACCOUNT WHAT HE DOES AND CONSIDER IF HE IS LABORING IN THE VINEYARD OF THE LORD."

St. Gregory the Great quoted in Christifideles Laici, 1988

SPIRITUALITIES

SPIRITUALITIES ARE PATHWAYS WITHIN the church tradition that lead us to the norms of Christ. The spiritualties of the St. Francis Altar Society are diverse, distinct, and deep. Over the years they have consisted of devotional practices, especially that of Eucharistic Adoration, participating in Corpus Christi processions, and society and parish rosaries and novenas, along with all of the liturgies of the church. Members of the Altar Society are devoted to the church and many are members of several other ministries. Many are daily communicants, assist in bringing communion to the sick, and attend funerals and rosaries of members and parishioners. Prayers for the deceased and the ill are an integral part of every Altar Society meeting and we consider this a valid and valued ministry that builds the mystical body of Christ.

The corporal and spiritual works of mercy of the St. Francis Altar Society weave an unbroken thread throughout their history as seen in their generous Christmas gifts to the mentally ill, clothing for those who were destitute, food and milk for the hungry, gifts to the U.S. soldiers in Vietnam during the Vietnam War, and on-going monthly food collections for the St. Vincent de Paul store. As documented in the Social Justice chapter, the minutes are replete with notes of the society's generosity, awareness, and concern for those in need within and well beyond the parish.

Some of the more popular and pervasive spiritualties of the group are described herein. They include prayers and writings, retreats, and devotions to *La Conquistadora* and the Blessed Sacrament. Individual spiritualities, faith sharing, and encounters are also narrated.

Prayers and Writings

A particularly prolific period of written spiritualties was shortly after the presidency of Mrs. Lyle Quintana Johnson in 1975–1976. From 1977 to 1983, she wrote numerous "meditations" for the Altar Society meetings on the lives of the saints, historical reflections, and seasonal holidays and liturgical holy days. Some of her meditations are incorporated throughout this book as insight into the Altar Society, its history, and spiritual legacy.

It was not until 87 years after its founding, in 2012, that the Altar Society adopted its official *Altar Society Prayer*, written by myself, President Skya Abbate. Thereafter, I also wrote several other prayers for the Sacred Heart League, the Liturgy Committee, and for the Altar Society for our retreats and meetings. Some of them can be found throughout this book at the start of many chapters.

The inspiration behind the *Altar Society Prayer* deserves mention on the power of prayer and its role in our lives and the society. The timing of the composition of the prayer was no coincidence. In 2012, the society was experiencing many tensions with a change in rector and when virtually all parish staff left or was replaced. These changes initiated the ensuing "flower wars."My preaching to the membership wasn't working in a parliamentary business meeting particularly over the change in the custody of the flowers.

It was hard to arrive at consensus or even have a civil conversation when whispers and strong feelings detracted from the order of the discussion. While I tried to make the meeting a safe place to vent, as that venting had to be done, sides were taken and it was difficult to adopt a stance of peace.

Deeply disturbed by the monthly feelings of irresolution that would remain after the meeting and wear on me until the next month, I wrote the prayer incorporating within it the mission of the society and most importantly its spirit of service. For me it was as simple as this: "We are called to do what we are asked to do." Some agreed and saw it this way. When the prayer was proposed and introduced I truly believed that the members understood the prayer. For the most part I saw a major shift occur in our way of thinking and in the frustrations of the group. This is not to say that no residual feelings persist for they do. Currently participation is extremely low when it comes to floral decorating for the holy days and members have told me they do not feel welcome doing so but for those who do this is not our perception.

By working with the Liturgy Committee and Art and the Environment Committee the Altar Society still has the special privilege of assisting in the preparation of the liturgical space, "of Cathedral quality," as beloved Monsignor Jerome Martinez y Alire taught us. We can still assist in decorating the church with the flowers. Now we are invited to work with others, including our new rector, Fr. Adam Lee Ortega y Ortiz, and his impeccable understanding of the connection between liturgy, environment, and floral art. Additionally, we can promote human flourishing and peace by getting over this hurdle. As St. Francis of Assisi learned, the voice to "the call to the altar" is not our own.

Retreats

The annual retreat, a classic Roman Catholic venue, was an integral feature of the Altar Society beginning in 1960, if not earlier. Retreats were attended by the members and usually included a priest who gave a spiritual presentation. At some point the retreats ended. They were recently reintroduced in 2008 to connect us more deeply in our ministry. They continue to this day and are a spiritual highlight of our year.

Our annual retreat consists of Mass where many participate as altar servers, gift bearers, readers, Extraordinary Ministers of Holy Communion, sometimes musicians, but always disciples. Here, the members re-dedicate themselves to ministry by reciting the *Altar Society Prayer.* The group informally has adopted the hymn "Let Us Go to the Altar of God"[1] as our signature song. At the annual retreat the members may process to the altar singing that hymn. In the sanctuary members wash each other's hands or anoint them with oil and recite Psalm 90:17,"May the favor of the Lord our God be ours. Prosper the work of our hands! Prosper the work of our hands!" I think we understand through the work of our anointed hands that we act like a flowing, living river that consecrates and nourishes a small piece of our desert community of faith.

Lunch offers an opportunity for nourishment, socialization, and fun. It is followed by a retreat presentation for about an hour on a topic that is carefully crafted by the President as the retreat leader to connect the theme to the work of the society or to introduce a new spirituality.The topics we have explored so far have included the following.

Retreat Topics

- Prayer, the Language of the Holy Spirit
- The Practical Theology of Grace
- St. Ignatius' Spiritual Exercises
- St. Therese of Lisieux of the Child of Jesus and the Holy Face: The Little Way in the Modern World
- Exodus 16:1–36, From Chaos to Communion—Manna: Heavenly Bread, Holy Word, and the Sabbath for Our Time
- Reflections on the Future: Working Meeting for the 2021 Anniversary
- The Incarnation, Imagination, and the Kingdom through the Ignatian Examen

An example of a retreat topic and its connection to the Altar Society was that of St. Therese of Liseux. St. Therese, known for her "little way," a mode of being, in which she wrote that whatever one does in love is more important than the bigger things one might equate with success and meaning, was a theme at our 2015 annual retreat that resonated with the members. One could construe that cleaning the church, washing and ironing the linens, or even decorating are nice but little things. Yet in each other's eyes and

1. Schutte, *Let Us Go.*

experience, in those gestures, the members are silent, unseen, small, and do these things out of love. In essence, I believe that the Altar Society must perform its ministry in the spirit of Therese's little way of love.

La Conquistadora

Figure 24 Tradition, The *La Conquistadora* Statue

As seen in the chapter on History, *La Conquistadora* plays a central role in parish life.

Mrs. Lyle Quintana Johnson wrote in 1983 on the parish's devotion to *La Conquistadora* in the following meditation.

> The oldest devotion to our Lady is in the shrine of *La Conquistadora*, the Lady of the Conquest. The diminutive charming stature of the *Conquistadora,* once beautifully carved out of willow wood and never meant to be in clothes, is steeped in antiquity having been brought to the Villa of Santa Fe in the Kingdom of New Mexico in 1625 from Mexico City by Fray Alonzo de Benavides. She represents the soul of the Hispanic southwest, its spirit of deep-rooted faith and unwavering devotion to Catholicism, even though her reign has seen some violent and troublesome times. Still today, as in ages past, Our Lady of the Conquest captures the hearts and souls and delivers them into the hands of her Divine Son.

President Skya Abbate recounts her connection to *La Conquistadora* in this narrative that she wrote for one of her courses in spirituality at Loyola University, New Orleans.

> At my church, the Cathedral Basilica of Saint Francis of Assisi, we have a statue, called *La Conquistadora*, Our Lady of Peace. The Cathedral is the oldest Marian shrine in the United States. Mary is greatly revered by various societies in the parish. She is processed through the church on certain occasions, and has a collection of clothes and jewels that are historically and liturgically appropriate. Miracles have been attributed to her since the 1600s, especially with her achieving peace between the Indians and the Spanish. Many of the women of the Altar Society are devoted to her and believe she has interceded in their lives and have testified to these miracles at our meetings. Recently our youngest member delivered her baby early and required a C-section. Strangely she contracted a flesh-eating bacterium in the hospital. The infection spread from her abdomen, to her thigh, and chest. She was administered the Sacrament of the Sick and basically was told there was nothing that could be done for her.
>
> The young woman, a lector at the parish and a photographer, had an especial devotion to Our Lady in this manifestation. On the day we heard her prognosis the biggest prayer group assembled at the church. We were shortly updated that the girl could be airlifted to another city to undergo treatment that offered some promise. She then began to get better and has since made a full recovery.

> You cannot tell the members of the parish, the young woman, or even myself that Mary did not save the life of our friend and Altar Society member.
>
> While personally I have devotion to Mary I really didn't relate to *La Conquistadora* as a statue. Yet when the woman was ill I did turn to Mary in this representation since I had purchased a framed photo of *La Conquistadora* done by the woman. I have it in a room in my house that I call my "Mary Room" as it has statues and photos of Mary in Italian, Chinese, Indian, Native American Indian, and Hispanic renditions. In the night I would get up and go into the room and look at the photo and plead with Mary to save our friend. I believe she did. Mary Jane Martinez, member and former President, recalls this story similarly. She claims that when the society prayed in Our Lady's chapel for the recovery of the girl it happened!

Another member, Helen Anaya, recounts a legend of *La Conquistadora.*

> When I was a child I remember my mother telling us a story about the *Conquisatadora* statue. When she was a little girl in the 1800s her Dad told her that on one of the Sundays they were going to begin the novena and procession from the Rosario Chapel to the Cathedral. The weather was unbelievable! It was pouring rain and the lightning and thunder would not stop. Since it was a promise to carry on with the novena, many men and women tried to lift the statue to carry it from the Rosario Chapel but the statue would not budge. My mother said that many people believed that the *Conquistadora* did not want to leave the Rosario Chapel, which was her original place of residency, or she was protecting her people from this terrible weather!

Blessed Sacrament Adoration

Promotion of Adoration of the Blessed Sacrament is part of the mission statement of the St. Francis Altar Society. Many members participate in this devotion on a regular basis and we report on attendance figures in one of our monthly meeting reports. We make sure that hours are attended so that the Blessed Sacrament is not left alone. We share this Adoration with the Nocturnal Adoration Society and the parishioners. While I might be mistaken, I have personally commented and still believe that Adoration is the best-kept secret of the Basilica. While the parish bulletin, a superb informational and educational publication, details many activities of our vibrant parish it does not announce when Adoration is or why it is done. I think that this is a deficiency that could be easily remedied as simply as putting a monthly reminder in the bulletin along with some short catechesis for established and new parishioners to remind them of this inconceivable opportunity. Just this month a small announcement had been placed in the bulletin by some of our members and hopefully that will continue with more information.

As part of the society's history, the members buy flowers for Adoration. In the 2000s, without knowing the past history, the members decided to purchase flowers or plants out of their own money for monthly Adoration except for Advent and Lent when we fast from flowers. This practice has been very popular as an Altar Society devotion and allows us to further work with our precious flowers for the praise and glorify of God.

Faith Sharing and Encounters

The Altar Society provides a natural forum for small group faith sharing experiences. They have emerged over the years in members recounting their struggles, difficulties, healings, and great joy in the experience of their faith. Some of these stories recorded in the history have been provided but countless more have not made their way into this written word. One particular example of a member's struggle with her faith was shared recently and is told herein.

Trials of Faith

Reflecting her spiritual orientation to ministry and life Mary Louise Giron, former President, shares the sadness and difficulty one can encounter as part of a people of God and the support derived from community. She writes,

> Death came calling in the form of cancer. The cancer was relentless and took one beloved life. Cancer was a cross to bear. It affected each and every one of us. My faith in God was like a wrestling match with doubt in my spiritual life. Despite the challenges and despair, God was there! I found strength in the love of family and in the warm embrace of friends. How beautiful a day can be when kindness touches your heart.

When sorrow comes, God's promises are shining rays of hope that break through cloudy skies to bring warmth and help us cope with the trials and tribulations in life. God gives us strength to weather any storm. God will never leave us alone when skies are gray as long as we believe and trust. God was with me to hear my every prayer, to comfort and guide me. I was never alone. We never know when the call will come but faith is all we need to survive the great losses in this world.

The Peregrinos

Every year hundreds of men and women in New Mexico organized into separate troops of men and women walk hundreds of miles across the state for vocations. They have been doing this for at least forty years without fail. The weather conditions of New Mexico are quite diverse and severe in some places. It can alternate from unseasonably cold, colder in the mountainous terrain, at night 20–40 degrees cooler, ice, snow and hail, or unbearable heat, with hot, howling, dry winds.

The walkers engage in these environments, sleep beneath the stars, cook and walk, many times in silence or to the accompaniment of reciting the rosary or singing. A small medical team travels with them to care for blisters, heatstroke, insect bites and other wounds acquired on the way. The groups are organized into men and women and they alternate visiting us. They range in age from their teens into their sixties. The Saint Francis Altar Society is their host in Santa Fe at the virtual end of their trek. The event gets in the newspaper but more importantly into the hearts of the walkers and the ladies as our own independent liturgical/social event. No one wants to miss it.

The basic format of the event is an *encuentro* (a meeting/greeting/encounter) where their *Guia* and ours meet. A *Guia* is a crucified Christ, on a pole or cross that leads them in their journey along with Our Lady of Guadalupe. We meet them, have Mass or a service, prayer and song, and then we serve them lunch. During lunch we sit with them to learn about what their pilgrimage means. We have private talks about blistered feet and endurance and why they walk as a way to meet God.

After lunch, they bless us, we bless them, we have an exchange of gifts. Some song is sung in which we all participate and then they leave for rest, a shower, and dinner later in another church. Two days later all the pilgrims meet at the Sanctuario de Chimayo, the most famous place of pilgrimage in New Mexico, where many miracles have been performed through the holy dirt of the shrine. Crutches, wheelchairs, rosaries, prayers, photos, statues and testimonials of cures crowd the walls of the small room adjacent to the dirt pit and adjacent to the sweet rustic chapel adorned with the hand carved, naturally pigmented religious art of Northern New Mexico.

Many *encuentro* days are also a quintessential Santa Fe day of mild heat, a delicious breeze, unending blue sky and no smoke from the fires in the state or nearby states. Sometimes we assemble in the cool prayer garden to meet and rest at the station of Jesus in his tomb. We thanked them for what and how they do this walking prayer through the climates, in the weather and wilderness, which they choose as a way to encounter divine presence. We talk about our Catholic walk that all take and how we meet Jesus on the road be it Damascus, Emmaus, a long winding road, a rocky road, a dead end, or the a walk like theirs in the literal wilderness or the wilderness of life. The St. Francis Altar Society ladies love the *encuentro* we have with our brothers and sisters in faith as we reflect upon the significance of vocation in our lives and how we answer that call.

As we consider our spiritualities it is helpful to look for further guidance. St. Gregory the Great exhorts, "Keep watch over your manner of life, dear people, and make sure that you are indeed the Lord's laborers. Each person should take into account what he does and consider if he is laboring in the vineyard of the Lord.[2] This philosophy reminds the society that it is beckoned to blossom in service to the Church. We must remind ourselves that we are the Lord's laborers!

Margaret Wheatley, modern organizational expert, also reminds us that our behaviors and spiritualities I would contend are not only for us but have repercussions. She prompts, "We will never know how our small activities will affect others through the invisible fabric of our connectedness," or what she calls our "critical connections."[3] The society in its humble service touches many in mutual connectedness. Parishioners see this grace in the members and we surely find it in each other.

An example of that recognition is a poem written to the members by an active parishioner in 2017 who observed the works of the Altar Society. She writes,

2. John Paul II, *Christifideles.*

3. Wheatley, *Leadership*, 45.

So many times I see you
Like angels whispering by
Dusting this, shining that,
Like angels in the sky!
Behind the scenes you scurry
To be sure the poor are fed
Delivering goods to those in need
And never a word be said.
It is never enough to say indeed,
Thank you for your every deed!"
But this I know and it should be said,
God bless the Altar Society one and all
For you have heard our Father's call.
Thank you for keeping our holy place alive
With your selfless, giving love.
In Christ, Mary Richman

While not exhaustive, these practices are some of our humble, simple, labor of love and "little ways" that encompass spiritualties that nourish the members of the St. Francis Altar Society, the parish, and Mystical Body of Christ.

Figure 25 Sister Emilia Atencio

10

The Personalities

Mentors, Priests, and Rectors

"I AM YOURS—HEART, BODY AND SOUL."

Monsignor Jerome Martinez y Alire to the St. Francis Altar Society, 2000

OVER THE YEARS THERE have been many special people who have influenced the St. Francis Altar Society. It is not surprising that most of them have been priests due to the intimate connection of the Altar Society with the functions of the parish and the care of the church. All of these rectors served as the Spiritual Director of the society since they were considered officers from the very first Constitution. The rectors played a vital role in the Altar Society and worked very closely with the members as the chapter on the Years recounts. Over time it appeared with the priest shortage that the priests had less time to interface with the society in the last decade. However, it is also true that they trusted the women to do their work both independently and in concert with overall parish operations and that freedom to serve in our own defined way is cherished.

Retrospectively, looking at the historical documents, and in asking the current members about those who influenced them, the following people came to mind. However, this is an infinitesimal record of those mentors who impacted the spirituality and sociability of the Altar Society in their close to one hundred year legacy of faith and service.

FR. PAX SCHICKER, RECTOR AND SPIRITUAL DIRECTOR

If the surviving minutes and scrapbook teach us anything it is how beloved Fr. Pax Schicker was to the members of the St. Francis Altar Society. Likewise, his love of the Altar Society is evident in the minutes where he repeatedly thanked, praised, and instructed the women as the Spiritual Director of the society. He is hailed in numerous articles in the *New Mexican* newspaper for his attendance at Altar Society functions and his talks on liturgical topics to the membership.

Fr. Pax was born in Louisville, Kentucky in November 1907 and studied to be a Franciscan priest. He served as Associate Pastor at the Cathedral from 1934 to 1940 and then as rector from 1956 to 1963. In 1959 he gave informative talks on the symbolism of the priests' vestments, which the women of the Altar Society made, as well as the significance of the liturgical colors. On his 39th birthday a mammoth four-tier cake was presented to him at a surprise birthday party. He was so delighted at the gesture and joked that he would have preferred to remain like Jack Benny, ageless and discrete.

In 1962, generous Fr. Pax cooked a steak dinner exclusively for the ladies of the Altar Society. The meal featured his famous steak sauce, summer salads, bite size chile *rellenos*, rolls, punch and coffee. In their history, while they fed thousands, no one priest except our dear Lord ever fed them and it was a moment to savor.

In 1965, while assisting at a wedding at the Cathedral, Fr. Pax suffered a heart attack and died days later at the age of 57. The society and the Cathedral remember him for the restoration of the Blessed Sacrament Chapel and the beautification of the Rosario Chapel. The Altar Society regarded him as the quintessential Spiritual Director.

Fr. Reynaldo Rivera, OFM, Spiritual Director

Fr. Reynaldo Rivera served the archdiocese from 1953 and the Cathedral since 1975. He was greatly appreciated for his inclusive ministry to the young, old, and sick, as well as parents, Indians, Spanish and Anglos. He renewed many of the Santa Fe Fiesta traditions that give Santa Fe its unique culture and spirituality. He created an ambience where all races and cultures could come to the mother church and know they were coming home.

In 1982, he was cruelly murdered after responding to what he thought was a call from a person who needed the Sacrament of Anointing. At his death at the age of 57, thousands of people processed to the cemetery through the streets of Santa Fe praying the rosary. As a dedicated priest devoted to his religious community and God, he lived the life of St. Francis that so inspired his life.

Monsignor Jerome Martinez y Alire, Rector and Spiritual Director

As we have seen in the chapter on the Spiritualties, for members of the Basilica, *La Conquistadora* is not just a statue but also the veritable presence of Mary and a significant influence in the life of Jerome Martinez who was to become a Spiritual Director of the Altar Society.

At the age of 12 Jerome recounts that he attended the novena (a nine day commemoration) promised to Mary in exchange for the peace achieved between the Spanish and the Native Americans in 1717. Jerome claims that he received his call to the priesthood at that time.

At the early age of 13 he left home to study for the priesthood. He studied at St. Michael's High School, and then at the College of Santa Fe, where he majored in the history of the Southwest. He is considered an expert on the history of the Catholic Church in the Southwest. After his studies in the seminary he was ordained a priest on the feast of St. Joseph on March 19, 1976. At the age of 25 he was named Dean of Students at the Immaculate Heart of Mary Seminary in Santa Fe where he helped other young men in their vocations.

His first assignment as pastor was at the parish of El Rito, in a dilapidated 150-year-old church, that of *San Juan Nepomuceno.* He refused to tear it down and build a new church because he believed that these old missions spoke volumes of the values and sacrifices of generations. He saw to it that it was refurbished and preserved as a physical and spiritual fortress of faith.

After the restoration of the church, Fr. Jerome was ordered by the El Rito Archbishop to study at the Catholic University in Washington, D.C. There he graduated with honors earning a Pontifical License in Canon Law. He returned to Santa Fe and became Chancellor of the Archdiocese and moderator of the Curia. He directed an administrative reorganization, started the Archbishop's Commission for the Preservation of Historic New Mexico Churches, and founded the Catholic Task force on AIDS related ministries. He served as the Judicial Vicar for the Provincial Court of Appeals for the Marriage Tribunal.

In 1990, he was charged with founding a new church in Santa Fe, named *Santa Maria de la Paz.* Through the process he was adamant about giving credit to his beloved Santa Maria parishioners for the success of its existence. He tried to instill in the parishioners that it was their church and that he was there to help.

When the Franciscan presence of priests dwindled in Santa Fe, in 1999, then Archbishop Michael J. Sheehan chose tenth generation native son Fr. Jerome to be the rector of the St. Francis Cathedral, the mother church of all Roman Catholics in the Archdiocese of Santa Fe. He was the first non-Franciscan to serve as rector in 80 years and one of the few native Santa Feans to hold this position. One of the biggest challenges here was to refurbish the church including a thorough cleaning inside and outside of the old stones of which it was built along with preserving the original stained glass windows of the apostles imported from France when the church was constructed. This and more were done in preparation for the Basilica's 400th anniversary in 2010. He achieved changes to the Cathedral, physically and spirituality, which exceed the scope of this book.

Whether as Spiritually Director of the Altar Society, in his homilies, or administrative capacities, he inspired people to do their best. His connection to his parishioners was deep and enduring. He greatly influenced the Altar Society by empowering them to serve at the altar with both pride and humility.

Sr. Emilia Atencio, Sister of St. Dominic, Sacristan, Member and Mentor

In her own words Sr. Emilia tells us about her relationship to the Altar Society.

> My years as part of the Altar Society were very enjoyable and happy. I am grateful for all the work the Altar Society has done. I have been in many parishes and no other Altar Society has worked as hard as the St. Francis Altar Society.
>
> Some of the most memorable events of the Altar Society are our wonderful meetings and when we decorated the church. My brother, Isaac, would bring us branches of Crown of Thorns from a plant, and the women enjoyed decorating the church with them

for Lent. She adds in connection with her work as a docent, people can't believe that *La Conquistadora* was carved in the 14th century. They just think I'm making it up when I tell them.

I am most proud of all the Presidents of the Altar Society. Credit should be given to the Presidents and to Skya because she has served for so long. They have all worked so hard to make us successful. I am most grateful to them and all who contributed their ideas and hard work for the dinners of the parish. Their influence is greatly appreciated!

I'd like to commend Olinda Garcia for being Treasurer for 18 years and who has kept the Altar Society in good financial order. She has been in charge of the money and has done such excellent job. I always felt the women of the Altar Society were extremely dedicated to the church, and did so much work with dinners, decorating, linens, and whatever was needed. My experience was that they tried their very best to serve the parish wherever they could or wherever they were needed.

Bless all the great women who have been so dedicated and who have worked so hard. I am so grateful that you haven't forgotten me and even asked me to contribute to the book. I am looking forward to reading about 100 yrs. of faithful service. May God bless you and all your dedicated work!

Olinda Garcia, Altar Society Treasurer, 2000–2018

Olinda likewise recounts her involvement with the Altar Society.

I began learning about the St. Francis Altar Society when I was a young girl. My mother, Lucy Barreras and my aunt, Matianna Taylor were active members of the society. I remember many meetings and Silver Teas at my house, my aunt's, and at the Governor's mansion. The members always dressed their best and many wore beautiful hats. My aunt had the most beautiful silver bowl and ladle that were used only for these Silver Teas.

Many years later, shortly after I retired from state government, I decided to take a new perspective and joined several ministries at the Cathedral. One of these was the St. Francis Altar Society (1997–present).Here I found a group of ladies who had a rich history of devotional life and love within the parish church. When I joined, the Altar Society made up the core of sacristans, forever bustling about the sacristy. The spiritual component bound the group of ladies in the parish. Through our dues, donations from members, parishioners, and our hands, hearts, and body we accomplished our purpose.

I always hope that we can co-ordinate not just sacristy duties and linen schedules to continue this most important ministry and to help other ministries when solicited. We do it with the love of our church and above all for the love and praise of God. I invite a new generation of women and men from the parish to join us. The St. Francis Altar Society is a dynamic group of close friends who support our parish community and we have a little fun along the way!

The St. Francis Altar Society lovingly remembers and honors these significant mentors of our society. So many gave us their unique presence, strength, and foresight that have made us a society and are integral to our relationships with each other, the parish, and the world.

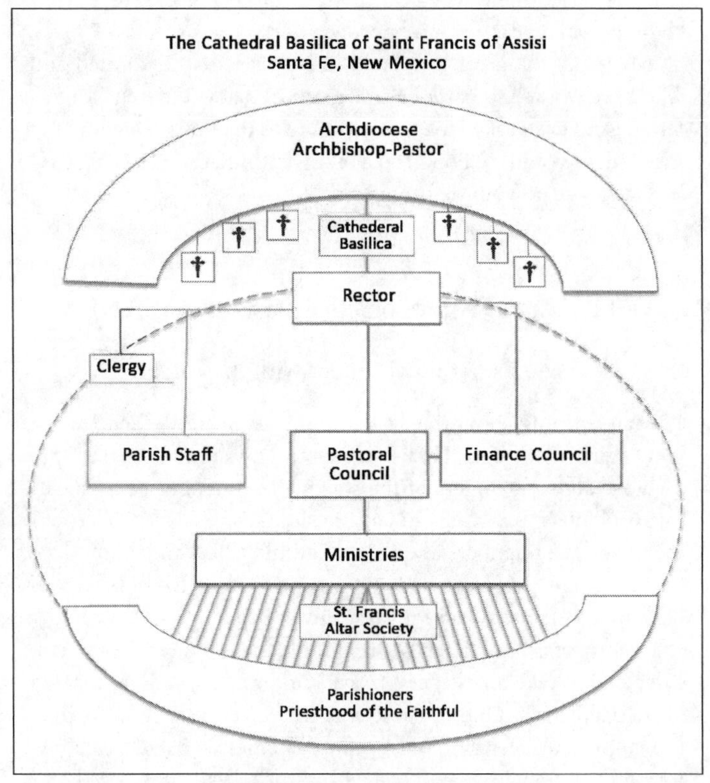

Figure 26 Organizational Flow Chart

11

Organizational Analysis

The Invisible Field of Interconnectedness

"We are like a field of wild flowers growing together and made more beautiful by our diversity and differences, our fruits, our blossoms, and even our natural decline."

Skya Abbate, President, 2005–2018

OVERVIEW OF ORGANIZATIONS

At this one-hundred-year juncture, it is fruitful to analyze the institution of the St. Francis Altar Society to absorb the lessons that come with learning and experience. Evaluation tools such as organizational theories, membership surveys, Roman Catholic traditions and spiritualties can assist in identifying the society's strengths and weaknesses, and what works and what does not work, in order to guide the society as an institution into the future. Lessons for other ministries likewise may be learned.

Institutions are ways in which cultures organize their goals to accomplish certain tasks. Ideally these goals aid the community in which they are embedded. Most cultures have five major institutions—the family, educational, political, economic and religious institutions—in rudimentary or highly bureaucratized forms. The Altar Society is primarily a religious one, designed to aid the community with which it identifies. Like most organizations, its mission, leadership, and membership characterize the society. As a voluntary organization it faces the issues of commitment and sustainability. Each of these facets, including their strengths and weaknesses, deserves exploration as part of its organizational analysis. Firstly, before these dimensions can be plumbed, the lens of the nature of voluntary organizations is helpful in offering organizational insight into the St. Francis Altar Society.

Voluntary organizations

Voluntary organizations are a hallmark of democratic societies. As such, America has many thousands of voluntary organizations that are based upon free and non-coercive membership. The church too relies upon the free association of lay people organized into ministry to accomplish its many tasks and the goals and missions they seek to achieve.

A particular strength of voluntary organizations is that members can freely join them and likewise, they can freely exit. The motivations to join voluntary organizations fall into three categories. Firstly, a material or non-material benefit such as a spiritual interest may be one's motivation. Secondly, a particular need of the person such as a desire for sociability may be another. Thirdly, effectual or ideological reasons such as identification with a cause or mission may be a reason. In a voluntary organization it is the person who decides which organization they might join and why.

The challenge of voluntary organizations in search of meeting their goals is that they need to attract members to the group and then to have mechanisms to keep their members once they have joined. They also need to be able to cultivate leadership to get the work done. Thus, it is helpful for the organization to understand what motivates people to join, participate, and remain in the organization. These motivations need to be sustained by the organization. This is primarily achieved by the member being socialized into moral involvement. As a result, a voluntary organization has two primary mechanisms to meet their goals and to be sustainable:solicitation and socialization.

Solicitation refers to recruiting members. This can be done through advertising and visibility. Each organization must choose how to solicit or recruit. Generally something must be done to bring in new members for the organization to meet its goals and to survive. An interesting characteristic of Americans is that they tend to join voluntary organizations. Americans like causes but their involvement may be more circumscribed as we shall soon see. Recent statistics reveal that American volunteerism is on the decline in the United States.

Commitment building is achieved through socialization mechanisms. In contrast to coercive organizations that use physical force to get members to do things or utilitarian organizations that offer rewards and punishments to meet their goals, voluntary organizations rely upon the internalization of norms and identification with authority as the basis of their power. Just as Americans freely join voluntary organizations, it is noted that Americans are good at giving of their money to the organization but not of their time because of alternate interests. "Side-bets" are activities that compete with the members' time. This is true more than ever in today's economy when families must work longer hours to get by. This necessity vies for the members' valuable time. This lens on the nature of voluntary organizations carries over into church organizations and ministerial involvement.

ORGANIZATIONAL FEATURES: MISSION, MEMBERSHIP, LEADERSHIP, COMMITMENT, AND SUSTAINABILITY, STRENGTHS AND WEAKNESSES

Mission

Care for the house of God and its inner sanctum is the privileged task of an altar society. Analysis of the historical documents that detail the work of the society in minutes, agendas, correspondence, Presidents' annual reports, and interviews revealed that the care of the altar, sacristies and the sanctuary, devotion to the Blessed Sacrament, promoting the spirituality of the membership and parish sociability are the primary goals of the society that endure to this day. In both overt and understated ways, the hierarchy of the church and the parish allow, encourage, and support the Altar Society in its work according to principles of solidarity and subsidiarity.

Clearly the structure of the St. Francis Altar Society has succeeded for almost 10 decades and will continue. Its mission has served as a light to illumine that path. There is irrefutable testimony that women will come forward to care for the church. At this historical juncture, the foremost goal of the society is to cultivate leadership followed by increasing membership.

Membership decline is not uniquely endemic to this Altar Society but is a sociological trend in today's church and in a busy culture. For instance, some societies have renamed themselves Women's' Clubs to attract members.[1] No doubt the Cathedral Basilica of St. Francis of Assisi Altar Society will endure, however it may need to scale back some activities and/or reinvent itself to adjust to changing times and membership levels. If membership becomes invigorated and grows, that service can continue its trajectory to expand beyond the physical altar. From my perspective, it seems that a key to this growth may rest not only in increased membership numbers but also in a transformation of the member's identity from that of a volunteer and member to a minister and disciple just as the society frames itself as a ministry. Sometimes the day-to-day work, even drudgery, obscures seeing discipleship as ministerial love over work.

This reframing can be done through the power of language, how we reference ourselves, and how we interpret the altar. Language is a powerful vehicle for describing, shaping, and influencing our mental models of reality. Language has the power to generate or destroy. Through a cycle of conversation and continuous reflection our mental models have the personal and cultural value of making our experiences and tastes of reality fuller than we could ever dream of alone as we enter into the universe of possibility and conversion —indeed God's dream.

Mental models or assumptive frameworks, and the language of metaphors are lenses through which we see and organize the world.[2]No single lens reveals the fullness or nature of reality, however, like a good pair of glasses, some lenses can improve our sight if it is impaired. The concept of'the primacy of the whole" is one lens with which to view the world, a world of *communio* or interrelationships.

The primacy of the whole suggests that the nature of the self, of the person, and of the organization is communal and thus relational. Community becomes the vortex of individual as well as group growth, maturation, and development. This mental model is not only empowering to each individual person but to the group as a whole. When the organization acknowledges the primacy of the whole we can see our story though a new prism.

1. Langlois, *Parish Altar Societies.*
2. Hawkins, *The Learning*, 28.

We can learn through listening, sharing, and history. In short, we need each other for transformative life and the actualization of the organization.

This richer institutional context of community implies that the whole is more important than a part of an organization. This concept directly derives from a "living systems model of life." In many ways this concept is consonant with St. Paul's theology of the Body of Christ wherein all parts work together for the fullness of the life of the church. These dual frameworks of the primacy of the whole, and a seeing the organization as a living system, take us out of our individual or even group, silo mentality and into a world of open fields, horizons, and possibilities. Fences are broken down and relational interaction can vitalize the dynamic potential of human and organizational diversity. The St. Francis Altar Society, through conscious organizational analysis, has the priceless opportunity to expand the assumptions of our mission statement into a broader vision of self, church, community and world. We have the chance to serve the altar of the world by viewing our group as part of the larger world. This whole picture fosters our own growth and helps us solve our problems and cultivates a consciousness of generativity and love that is the foundation of our motto—"A labor of love for the glory of God."

Membership

Enduring membership for close to 100 years is a formidable accomplishment for any organization and the St. Francis Altar Society has succeeded in this domain. They have met their mission, enjoyed each other's company, and as some have noted, even have had some fun along the way!

Real challenges exist for the Saint Francis Altar Society with declining participation and membership due to age, infirmity, or disinterest. Since we are a voluntary organization, these are potential vulnerabilities that are impacting the future of the group. While the recidivism rate is low, and the society is able to attract a few new members a year, a more energetic presence in the parish and a formal recruitment process must be undertaken. See Table 2 and the membership graph, Figure 27 that illustrates membership levels.

Table 2. Membership 1975– 2018

1975	137
1976	139
1977	122
1978	155
1979	142
1980	142
1981	140
1982	154
1983	154
1984	157
1985	181
1986	165
1987	184
1988	192
1989	201
1990	184
1991	178
1992	169
1993	151
1994	---
1995	145
1996	135
1997	102
1998	119
1999	131
2000	120
2001	126
2002	139
2003	-
2004	143
2005	138
2006	135
2007	114
2008	110
2009	134

2010	-
2011	-
2012	-
2013	90
2014	86
2015	75
2016	81
2017	75
2018	76

Note: Membership numbers include honorary members. These numbers were higher in the 1980s.

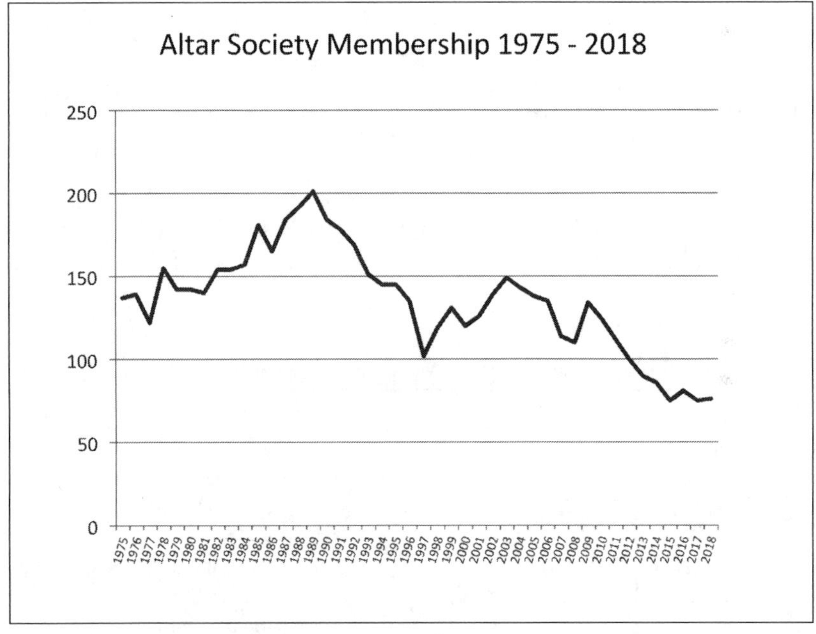

Figure 27 Membership graph

It is interesting to note from the minutes that regardless of the number of members in the society, that over time, approximately 25 members attended meetings and did most of the work so the apparent decline in membership numbers need not be alarming but interpreted.Additionally, based upon sociological trends found by the Pew Research Center, while the number of Catholics is increasing in the United States from 48.5

million to 76.7 million between 1965–2014, the number of Catholics who reported attending Mass at least weekly fell by nearly half from 47% to 24% between 1974–2012. If a quarter of Catholics are going Mass, overall there are significantly less people to draw from to fill the ministries. Also within parishes there are new ministries proliferating to serve the whole person in their daily-lived faith.[3] Thus, while fewer members are in the Altar Society, there is no reason for alarm but rather appreciation for those who do serve. Nevertheless to share the richness of our ministry, in response to these trends, a Membership Committee has been reinstated in 2017 and goals for the year have been identified, articulated, and already implemented. The plan is expressed as an action plan and is already working as proof that planning works.

Membership Committee 2018 Action Plan

Mission: The primary purpose of the Membership Committee is to increase membership in the St. Francis Altar Society of the Cathedral Basilica of St. Francis of Assisi so that the society may fulfill its mission. Secondarily, it serves as a vehicle of communication with parishioners and parish staff on the works of the society. The Membership Plan is summarized in this Table 3.

Table 3. The Membership Committee Action Plan

Goals	By Whom	When	Achieved	Notes
Have Masses said and published in the parish bulletin for the living and deceased members of the St. Francis Altar Society	Treasurer	Twice a year — in February and August.	Has been implemented and was changed to March and September 2018 due to availability of the parish Mass schedule	Keep doing

3. Lipka, *The Number of U.S. Catholics.*

Recommend that members wear aprons, ribbons, and name tags when cleaning and decorating the church and when hostessing to create visibility	All	Immediately Start with the March Chrism reception 2018	Started	Continue
Create a brochure on our work	Skya and Membership Committee	After the completion of the book		
In the parish bulletin describe what we do(summary) or other events	Skya and Membership Committee	March 2018	Done and new member joined	Continue
Update website	Skya	After the completion of the book 2018		
Invite former members back	a. President in annual membership letter	February 2018	Done	Keep doing
	b. Members verbally to each other			
Target presentations to groups	As invited or initiated	Any one	Skya had done yearly for five years, did in May 2018 to the new members of the church	
Set membership goals for 3 years	5 new members a year			
Bring one guest to one meeting	All who can	As possible		

Leadership

While the overarching way to meet mission may be the mechanisms of a relatable mission and sufficient membership as described above, Peter Senge's notion of personal mastery is relevant to the leadership of the society and is helpful to determine the continued vitality, vibrancy, and viability of the Altar Society. According to Senge,[4] personal mastery is the spiritual foundation of learning organizations and all organizations that hope to survive must learn. Personal mastery consists in the development of an organizational member's vision and competencies to accomplish that vision. The leader's task is to help develop those opportunities that foster the self-development of others and the cultivation of gifts for the work and good of the whole, not simply as a move towards individual self-actualization.

A leader must be authentic and credible for members to follow. A leader needs to be a good communicator. A leader can do so by being a better listener who can hear the sides of an issue and can respond to it with flexibility and creativity. Through active listening a leader must be a minister, servant, facilitator, harmonizer, peacekeeper, and reconciler. A leader must synthesize positions and then lead the group into action. A leader must be the taskmaster who gets things done, and the socio-emotional leader who can smooth over conflicts with resurrection-like transformation. A leader must wield power but that power should engender, empower, and embrace the connections for the members. Visions need to be articulated and those visions conveyed and captured by the group. St. Francis of Assisi, our patron saint, was wonderfully present to every person he met. He is good mentor of leadership. In many ways the leader must be like Francis, the veritable grain of wheat that falls on the ground and dies.

Through sharing we grow in personal sanctification and engage in deeper learning about our church and the world. This is a challenge the officers, particularly the President, and individual members must master in calling forth leadership. While good leaders are necessary, members may become dependent upon leaders for their skills. If the leaders are entrenched for too long the organization may fail to grow, stagnate, and even die. As mature adults we must cultivate and practice personal mastery for the good of the whole over our individual stakes and this entails members being willing to share in leadership responsibilities.

Commitment

The society's organizational strengths are many because of its longevity, the clear focus of its mission, the inspiration of their leaders and the commitment of the members. The frequency of monthly meetings buttresses the mission, structures the work, and reinforces the faithful commitment of its

4. Senge quoted in Fleischer, *The Ministering*, 108.

members. These meetings provide opportunities for prayer and networks for the members to interface with each other as whole persons and with other mediating structures such as the Pastoral Council, the Liturgy Committee, and the rector through Spiritual Direction. Socialization processes such as reading the *Altar Society Prayer,* and rededication to the mission at the annual retreat, are mechanisms that unite the members. These are powerful ways for the members to become reacquainted with the mission, re-socialized into moral involvement, and realigned with each other as equal members empowered to do the work of the society.

Our mission statement acknowledges what industrial psychologists have learned—that the human being is a highly social being with an emotional life that is valuable in the workplace.[5] This idea can be carried over into ministry. Ministry is not a closed or mechanistic Newtonian system, but one with interconnections that value the whole and the whole person, including spiritual growth, and community development. Our organizational success is linked with the very real roots and personal interconnections that we have made with each other—roots that are anchored in our deep, spiritual, interpersonal relationships. As such, members enjoy the social and spiritual support afforded by their membership in the society. It is my experience that the more spiritual and social practices we integrate into our ministry the greater membership satisfaction.

Sustainability

Change is certain in life. Life is learning and organizations must learn as well. A learning organization is one that is continually expanding its capacity to create its future.[6] Learning organizations are structures"where people continually expand their capacity to create the results they truly desire, where new and expansive patterns of thinking are nurtured, and where collective aspiration is set free, where people are continually leaning how to learn together."[7] As we have seen, the nature of the Altar Society is not static, even though some would prefer it to remain so. Its nature is to be as flexible as the palms that welcomed Jesus into Jerusalem, bowing willingly, freely, and expansively to a reality greater than our own.

5. Fleischer and Gast, *Pastoral,* 11.
6. Senge quoted in Fleisher and Gast, *Pastoral,* 71.
7. Senge quoted in Fleisher and Gast, *Pastoral,* 71.

Every social organization has its tensions, conflicts, and opportunities that must be faced in order to progress to a more mature stage of communal life and vision. While overwhelmingly the ministry of the St. Francis Altar Society is achieving its stated mission and goals through its shared vision and harmonious way of working together, it is not immune to conflict or weaknesses. If there are varying points of view on expenditures, or what to serve at a meal, or our perspective on the flowers, the society should strive to work it out through consensus. This conversation is healthy and needs to be encouraged. The members are invited to use prayerful discernment in order to tackle any deeper challenges and not to be discouraged by what is indeed the functionality of conflict. The trials of work, ministerial involvement, and expenditure of energy actually sanctify the world. Organizational specialists note, "In conflict, as anywhere, God's perspective would call us to humility and service and to true justice instead. With this mindset, we can begin to view conflict as an opportunity to follow our baptismal call rather than as the dismal situation it would seem to be at first."[8]

The society is very efficient and would like others to be the same! For instance, some things that would help on occasion would be earlier, better, and faster communications with other parish constituencies. Communication between parish staff and ministries could flow more smoothly. However, without telling others what to do, this is our test—to be patient, co-operative disciples.

Meeting mission requires work in the form of reflection, reconciliation, and renewal. The society's weaknesses are challenges that can foster growth through conversations about leadership and power, infusion of new members and their gifts, and the ability to learn the territorial mental models of each other and other groups. Organizational expert Margaret Wheatley reminds us that just as no subatomic particle exists independent of its participation with other particles, so too is organizational life connected.[9] Conflict creates a vital opportunity for us to learn, grow, cooperate, serve the parish, and develop greater clarity. We are called to change, convert, reconnect and recommit to the meaning of our work. Lessons can be learned from conflict and its healthy resolution.

In my opinion, the Altar Society, like hearty desert flowers, blooms in abundance and adversity in unique constellations of beauty. We are like a field of wild flowers growing together and made more beautiful by our

8. Gaffney and Sortor, *Conciliation*, 184.

9. Wheatley, *Leadership*, 163.

diversity and differences, our fruits, our blossoms, and even our natural decline. Our weaknesses, or chaos, as Wheatley says, are momentary occasional slips that create the need for new meaning.[10]At these times it is good to remind ourselves of our unique identity by looking to our guidepost of service, that is our mission, and our patron, St. Francis of Assisi, and how he did things—with joy and humility. This strategy is what Fleischer and Gast recommend when they say, "In organizations, a well-claimed sense of mission draws energies back to the system's central purpose, even though structures, personnel, and programs may swirl and change."[11] "If a system is in trouble, it can be restored to health by connecting it to more of itself.[12] Another mechanism for realignment, in addition to mission and mentorship, is through Eucharistic Adoration and reception as our primary ways for literal and spiritual communion.

In order to understand how to survive, it is useful to look at where we have been, what we have done, and what promotes sustainability. An ecological context is an illustrative model for appreciating how to understand where a change in one part impacts the whole and how to survive through adaptation. So too it is through ministry that learning happens, faith is deepened, and critical community connections are established. This quantum model shifts emphasis away from an unchanging reality to a much more dynamic and relational one.[13] Einstein never had our group in mind as he explored his ideas about relativity yet his theory has organizational validity. The society is a power, not a place, an influence, not a destination.[14] It acts as a lay member organization and subculture. Like other ministries, it "helps us see the world differently with new vistas, new dreams and ways of imagining."[15] Our adaptive nature has ensured our survival as a long-standing ministry of sacramental love. To be sustainable we need to generate an "invisible field,"[16] an energy of loving service, drawing others into our vortices, like bees to the nectar, as Jesus did through his authority.

We are a living, learning organization that has survived due to a clear mission and yet we are challenged to remain flexible and to adapt

10. Wheatley, *Chaos.*

11. Fleischer and Gast, *Pastoral,* 205.

12. Wheatley, *Leadership,* 145.

13. Fleischer and Gast, *Pastoral,* 113.

14. Wheatley, *Leadership,* 55.

15. Osborne, *Orders,* 197.

16. Wheatley, *Leadership,* 53.

to changing times. The person of pastor/rector is the primary factor that affects the experience of the parish[17] and this without a doubt is how many parishioners experience the parish. Likewise, as a society, many are learning how to cope with that through considered discussion on the rector's ideas about church environment and his role in our organization. For instance, in terms of floral decoration, *The Constitution on the Sacred Liturgy* that has been in effect since 1963 simply says that noble beauty rather than mere sumptuous display should be the norm for sacred use (#351).[18] The rector understands this norm and so should we although not all agree. Catechesis is a must for understanding many issues.

The following model, adapted from a model of commitment building,[19] that I devised in my Masters thesis on voluntary organizations is offered as a way in which to build commitment and promote sustainability in an Altar Society

A Model of Commitment Building for a Successful Altar Society

1. The organizational structure should offer the potential for participative decision-making. In this way, the member is made to feel that she/he has some personal influence in the organization, thus identification with the organization is enhanced.
2. The structure of the Altar Society should be such that it offers the opportunity for the satisfaction of psychological and social needs such as can be attained through small group interaction. These situations allow the individual to get involved in the organization on a more personal level and to have the chance to relate to other people in a meaningful way. This is a good example of the importance of teams and committees to structure the work.
3. The organization should institute an effective socialization system, which orients the incoming members to the goals of the Altar Society, rather than to only the mechanics of the group. This type of socialization aims at aligning the motivations of the members to the goals of the organization. For instance a membership packet with the

17. Sweetser and Forster, *Transforming*, 24.
18. Paul VI, *Constitution Liturgy.*
19. Abbate, *Commitment.*

Constitution and By-Laws could be helpful along with a copy of this book.

4. The members should be made to feel that their role in the Altar Society is important. This can be done in several ways. One such way is to stress the interdependence between members in an Altar Society. Another way is to keep meetings open so that members can have this avenue for input into the organization. An additional way is for the Altar Society to provide meaningful jobs for the members so that they feel that their time is not wasted and that they are making a valuable contribution to the Altar Society. Leadership positions, teams, and committees are effective ways to do this.

5. The members, not only the officers, should do the work of the organization. An Altar Society is more likely to be successful when the energy comes from inside the organization.

6. Although various organizational problems have resulted from the size of the organization, size need not necessarily be a problem as long as other organizational factors are manipulated to compensate for size. One such factor is making sure that there are ways for the individual to meet her/his social needs. Another way is for the organization to structure itself so that the work of the organization is distributed efficiently. The Altar Society may for example, be subdivided into committees of other smaller groups. Not only may the work of the organization become more manageable under such a system, but in addition, a sense of purpose and community may be further established. In such a way the individual will be protected from feeling isolated, anonymous, and alienated within the group.

7. The organization could decentralize its power not only for the sharing of work responsibilities but because of the social-psychological implications of this type of arrangement. Again the committee structure would assist in this.

8. The annual retreat is a further effort to re-socialize members and to re-familiarize them with the old and emerging goals of the organization. This retreat can also be vital in inspiring members and putting them in contact with the energy that is generated when the whole group comes together. Members can also get a sense of the whole organization and their place in it at this time.

9. The organizational structure should facilitate the free flow of information between the members of the organization, especially between the officers and the other members of the Altar Society. Open meetings also facilitate the transmission of information. Newsletters too are instrumental in keeping members in contact with the business of the Altar Society especially those who cannot come to the meetings.
10. Social events offered by the Altar Society, both planned and spontaneous, aid in the development of commitment to and moral participation in the organization for they help in building a community in which the members get to know one another on a level apart from that related to Altar Society business. Such events can encourage the people to look forward to working together when they have the opportunity to get to know each other better.
11. The physical environment of the Altar Society should be one that encourages social interaction. Not only should there be areas for interaction such as talking, relaxing, eating, etc., but the general atmosphere of the organization should permit one to feel at home and comfortable so that the individual does not mind being at the Altar Society meeting. Interaction in the Altar Society is likely to be increased when one does not have to compartmentalize his/her personality and put on "an Altar Society self."
12. The physical environment of the Altar Society should also be one which ranks high in the value scale of its members, be it efficient, clean, neat, relaxing, informal, or comfortable.
13. Because involvement is an emergent process, education could be done throughout the member's career in the organization. This education should focus upon the goals of the Altar Society, its history, and role so that the person can get a broader perspective of his/her involvement in the organization.
14. The most effective form of social control will be the one that is congruent with the goals of the organization. Therefore, an Altar Society, which a normative organization should emphasize, the use of normative control, that is, to instill in its members a sense of identification with the norms and values of the organization.
15. The organization should recognize that the individual comes to the organization with differing reasons and expectations. Although the

organization can attempt to alter the involvement pattern of the members through the manipulation of the factors outlined, it should also respect the values of the members and not criticize members for their degree or reasons for involvement.

16. The organization should present itself to its members in such a way that the members could come to see the organization as good in itself and not just as a vehicle for the fulfillment of personal needs.
17. The broader the scope of the organization, that is the more activities the organization sponsors which permeate the extra-organizational life of the participants, the more likely the individual can meet many needs within the organization such that loyalty and commitment to the organization is increased. An increased scope may succeed in decreasing the influence of the larger social environment by reducing side-bets that the individual might make outside of the organization.
18. The greater the pervasiveness of the organization, that is the degree to which the organization permeates the life of the participants, the greater the chances are that the individual will more closely embrace the norms of the organization. One such way to increase pervasiveness is for the organization to assign definite roles to the members, such as through committees, so the person does not feel ambiguous in terms of their role in the Altar Society. In order for the member to feel that the Altar Society is her/his own, they must see their part in the operation of the organization.
19. Selectivity, or specific criteria for membership, can act as a filter in rooting out people that the organization does not want in the organization. However, Altar Societies like other voluntary organizations do not have any criteria for membership that keeps people out of the organization, although the rector approves of members.Consequently, the Altar Society is virtually forced to accept anyone who comes to its door. In this case then, when selectivity is low, the organization must rely on other organizational variables in order to have some control over its members.
20. A normative organization requires two types of elites for organizational effectiveness. Instrumental elites are those who facilitate the work of the organization, especially the business part such as the officers. Expressive elites, usually the President or Spiritual Director on the other hand, work especially with the normative aspects of the

organization, that is it is the job of these elites to establish a rapport with the members and between the members and the parish staff. It is the task of these expressive elites to convey to the members the larger goals of the Altar Society and the spiritual message of the Altar Society. Consequently, it can be seen that an organization which is normative in nature will be more likely to be effective when its elites are both concerned with the instrumental and expressive goals of the organization.

21. The organization should make efforts to increase the integration of its members. One way in which this can be accomplished is through modifying consensus on the goals and direction of the organization. Consensus can be increased through socialization, communication, and increased participation in the Altar Society and through a broader scope, which occupies more of the life space of the members, and through the variables outlined herein.

Going Forward

Socio-culturally, the Altar Society has successfully melded at least two cultures and socioeconomic classes, and diverse ethnic backgrounds into a desert garden of raw beauty that imitates the cycles of the natural world in its growth, struggles, and fruition. We try to practice a poverty of spirit in our works for social justice within the state and the community. The parish, with its active membership and long historical past, operates as an important mediating structure of faith for the members. The socio-cultural context is prophetic of the kingdom of God when peace will be established with all races. It is salvific because no one ethnic group is chosen for salvation. Ministerial enactments and outreach are done for many. All are welcome to vital participation in the society. Modern day ministerial praxis in the vineyard of the Lord has inherent challenges that pose unique and divine opportunities for service, grace, and joy.[20]

We do and can act as a model to other parish ministries and the Archdiocese and we hope that this book will advance our model of service to the altar and ministry in general. Our work can be viewed as loving discipleship. The organization's success cannot be personality dependent, thus new leadership must always come to the fore. These are advantages that would

20. USCCB, *Co-Workers.*

benefit the Altar Society. By engaging in these steps such changes are feasible in the system's life and they are requisite for its sustainability.

Theologian Terry Veling aptly intuits, "I believe that the Church in America is faced with the challenge of recapturing the Catholic vision of reality and presenting it in an engaging and imaginative way which markets any number of recipes for human fulfillment."[21] The Altar Society plays an important role in this interpretative task for others and now for ourselves as we reinvent and reposition our society in this modern era in an imaginative way. For instance, magisterial teachings such as *Christifideles Laici*[22] assure us, "The 'world' thus becomes the place and the means for the lay faithful to fulfill their Christian vocation because the world itself is destined to glorify God the Father in Christ." The Altar Society is a place to practice lay incarnational spirituality. Everything we do has an effect upon the members, the parish, the community, and the world in advancing the Incarnation. We need to convey this to others to be sustainable.

In an impromptu exercise the members recently were asked to use one word to describe the Altar Society. Overwhelmingly those words were interrelated. They were mostly "service" followed by synonyms of "dedication," and "perseverance." In ministry, we are instruments of the reign of God, making visible God's powerful love and presence.[23] This ministry of service, dedication, and perseverance is a "labor of love."

"True devotion," St. Frances de Sales says, "adorns and beautifies any vocation or employment."[24] Our true devotion is not expressed ultimately in floral decoration. Through our true devotion to the altar, friendships have been forged and faith renewed in the organization of the St. Francis Altar Society. I trust in the organic synthesis of the labor of love as a way to become saturated in the omnipresent love of God. It seems we know the sustainable spirit of our mission.

21. Veling, *Practical,* 60.

22. John Paul II, *Christifideles.*

23. Dues and Walkley, *Called.*

24. Dreyer, *Earth,* 46.

Figure 28 Morning Song

IN THE MORNING YOU SHALL SEE THE GLORY OF THE LORD

We are women of the desert
We love the heat and dryness
We welcome coolness and water
We see you in creation
The greenness of trees and grass
A clear blue sky, the crystal clouds
We know you in the new morning
You feed us with your wisdom
Your hand guides our work all day long
At night we give thanks for your presence
Our lives are never barren with you on our mind
We strive not to murmur only to give quiet thanks
We lay down our lives for others
We feed them with mercy and kindness
Give us your manna every day O Lord
And let us rest on your holy day in gladness. Amen.

by Skya Abbate

12

Goals and Dreams

The Lessons of History

"How Far We've Come, How Much We've Grown, How Much We Can Still Do"

Member, 2017 survey

WHERE WE HAVE BEEN

It is healthy and necessary for an organization to have goals and dreams as steps towards the fulfillment of its mission. Most businesses could not survive without them.Schools and colleges are required to have organizational goals. So too, voluntary organizations such as the St. Francis Altar Society could benefit from having institutional goals particularly in this time of aging, declining participation, and leadership. Goals are analogous to stepping-stones that lead one to the mission as illustrated in the goals listed in the Membership Action Plan found in the Organizational Analysis chapter. Goals are concrete plans on what to do, mapped out by personnel who will do them, and according to a timetable. With goals, the society can take a look at itself at the end of every year to see how it is progressing towards its mission.

In 2005, when I became the President, I took the liberty of distributing a simple impromptu survey at an Altar Society meeting to determine the possible direction the members might like to go in as an organization. The results revealed that the members noted the importance of devotion to the Blessed Sacrament and encouraged more devotion to First Friday Adoration. Members also wanted to see women continue to be allowed to hold leadership positions in the parish. In light of the fact that we are a tri-cultural community, some mentioned that they would like more Native American Masses as "it brings such a beautiful integration of the ancient traditions of Santa Fe." Also, "A parish hall complete with a kitchen" topped the list and understandably so since we have had a close relationship with food preparation and serving.

Other dreams, while idiosyncratic and not goals, are insightful of members' values. They also include desires not directly related to the society. Thus in 2018 they may no longer apply as the parish has achieved them or they do not fall under the scope of the Altar Society. Still they deserve mention of the thing members thought about.

- To have organ music at the 12 noon Mass
- A visit from the Pope
- For new parishioners to receive information, knowledge on the happenings, committees, and groups in the church
- Assign leaders to keep our family united and happy
- A better public address system
- More spirituality in this church
- Much more opportunity for small group faith sharing experience and spiritual support
- To have a priest in charge of Cristo Rey (a neighboring parish that the Cathedral tends) and to have at least three permanent priests at the Basilica who will be retained for a long time
- Since it is a Basilica and tourist attraction, we should have flowers on the altar all of the time. Many tourists have commented on how beautiful it looks and would like to take home ideas from the Basilica to their parishes. I don't think plain keeps your attentiveness to prayer only. It is beautiful to see the Lord's home displayed in all its beauty

- I would like to continue to have women in positions of Eucharistic ministers, Mass coordinators, readers, acolytes, etc. Women are good workers and good leaders and need to be able to serve and share their talents with the church, parish, and people of God.

It is interesting at this time that no mention was made of increasing membership, which in 2017, became the leading and most pressing goal of the society thus illustrating the need for goals and periodic, planned evaluation.

In 2017, in preparation for the start of this book, another questionnaire was distributed to all members in a mailed document. As summarized in the chapter on Mission slightly more than half of the members (51percent or 31 members) responded. While the questionnaire was anonymous this is about the same number of women who actively participate in the society by coming to the meetings and who clean and launder. The preponderance of the questionnaire was in a multiple-choice format. However, the final questions on goals, dreams, solutions, the importance of the Spiritual Director and history were framed as opened ended questions instead of leading questions to tap into those areas.

Interestingly, the response rate dropped dramatically with these questions. It is unclear why. Was it a physical difficulty that impaired writing such as arthritis? Was it symptomatic of membership disinterest, apathy, fatigue or satisfaction?Only 13 percent (7) of those who participated in the questionnaire commented on any goal. Four mentioned the need for increased and/or younger membership. Of those who answered, 100 percent(28) considered it important to know the society's history. Members commented that history is good and interesting. It could generate and provide information to new members. It could be informative and we could learn from it. Thus it could make us a better organization and foster deeper commitment. This is satisfying that members noted the function of history. Hopefully this book will help us learn, become better, and foster deeper commitment. This was certainly the case for the Spiritual Development and Writing Club who worked on this book.

Of those who answered 23 percent (12 or two-thirds) of the members thought it was important to have the rector as the Spiritual Director who would come to at least one meeting a year. The women were used to the Spiritual Director attending. Even though they felt the membership was spiritually healthy, a Spiritual Director could add strength to the organization and show respect to the women, and they felt that they would get to know about other things happening in the parish. Six members (11 percent or one-third) felt it would be nice to have him attend the meetings but that it was not necessary.

At the 2017 Altar Society Retreat, a working meeting was held to study the questionnaire results as the society moves towards its 100th anniversary. Subcommittees were established on the mission, membership, goals, dreams and solutions. The members of the subcommittees merged the goals and dreams together. These findings were then brought to the Spiritual Development and Writing Club as another subcommittee to discuss in the context of writing this book and to also make recommendations to the full membership. Over the course of four meetings that year these themes were discussed as part of New Business and acted upon. This was a four-fold functional structure: to gather data, to discuss it, to act upon it and to record it formally in writing in this book.

The main dreams that emerged were to increase membership, to have the Spiritual Director attend one to four meetings a year, and to keep our history recorded and alive. In 2018, a Membership Committee was formed to recruit members. The Spiritual Director will be purposely invited to meetings, and the history of the society has been written in this book!

Organizational Goals

It is my firm belief that dreams and goals are important. As the President and author who has long standing experience, perspective, and leadership expertise several ideas come to mind on future dreams that I believe will assist the society. They include the following.

1. To use this critical reflection as a training document for new officers.
2. To create a mentor system of past presidents.
3. To appoint an Altar Society Historian. Additionally to ensure the ongoing record of organization in a serious and accountable capacity with an actual job description just as the other officers have.
4. To serve as a model for other Altar Societies.
5. To pay attention to the quality and appropriateness of flowers, how they are grown, and where they come from so as to respect the earth and honor the mystery of God.
6. To reinforce the symbol of the altar as a holy place and Eucharistic table.

7. To promote membership as a "call to serve."
8. To continue to teach and reach out to parishioners and maintain sufficient membership to accomplish our tasks.
9. To emphasize the importance of Adoration for our society and parish.
10. To continue to do what are we doing well and analyze what could we do better.
11. To continue the frequency of meetings to reinforce our mission, distribute our workload, and provide opportunities for prayer and holiness for the members and the interface with the other mediating structures.
12. To promote a leadership style that is consistent with the love of Christ.
13. To revive writing of the annual reports. The historic annual reports should be composed by the President at the end of every calendar year and presented to the membership at the start of the New Year. This report can be put in the parish bulletin as a way to acknowledge the society's achievements, to promote visibility, and garner parishioner interest in the work of the group respectively. It may also increase membership. It should be published in the archdiocesan publication, *The People of God,* to let other Altar Societies learn about what the Cathedral Altar Society does. These reports can then serve as the basis for the compilation of ongoing history.
14. To formulate 3–5 year goals and assess annually.
15. To devise a membership questionnaire every five years to determine if the mission is being met, if the demographics have changed, how leadership and membership are progressing, and what are the new goals, dreams, and solutions. This survey will render data for long-range planning. Data from the questionnaire can be summarized and then planning can be done by having a frank discussion at our meetings or at an annual retreat. Long-range planning can be helpful in assessing the society's dreams and meeting its mission.
16. The Altar Society is given great freedom, latitude, and trust to chart its course under the organizational structure of the society and its relationship to the rest of the parish. We should cherish this independence and let it take us into new vistas of action.

17. As part of our ministry and mission, specifically the sanctification of the members, our ministry of older women faces many unique problems with health, income, and family problems. Members need assistance with their faith and the Altar Society can be one place to have it nurtured. Catholic adults need help to become adult Catholics. The bottom line is that faith intersects with every aspect of our lives and we all need the support of our faith in community for our spiritual development, which is the role of a parish. The Spiritual Director can assist in this need and we should include him in our works through invitation to meetings or by the articles we write for the parish bulletin. Alternatively, a representative to the Altar Society could be appointed by the rector to come to a meeting.

18. While not articulated as a society dream, as has been discussed in the chapter on Social Justice, social justice has been a longstanding operating principle of the St. Francis Altar Society. The mission of social justice is deeply embedded in the faith expression of the Roman Catholic Church. In fact, as the U.S. Bishops state in *Communities of Salt and Light, Reflections On the Social Mission of the Parish*,[1] "Parish social ministry is first and foremost a work of faith." That faith as expressed in the beatitudes and Jesus' words and deeds entails care for the least amongst us. While charity is a hallmark of Roman Catholic practice, I would still like to see a more conscious identification with social justice as an expression of gospel values and the fullest meaning of Eucharist served at the altar of the world.

19. In our parish we have about thirty ministries. The two that are most closely identified with social justice were the St. Vincent de Paul Society and the Peace and Social Justice Committee. Both provided clothing, food, money and other needs to the parish members and non-denominationally to the Santa Fe community. Their membership was very small, with about five to six members. About five years ago I heard from two friends who wanted to join the Peace and Social Justice Committee. They were told, "We don't need any more members." Yet, in my opinion, no person should be denied ministerial opportunity. There is unlimited work to be done in the social justice arena. New ideas should be entertained and new members should always be invited with open arms. In 2017, the Committee folded when it might

1. USCCB, *Communities.*

have survived and even thrived with new membership! This is a lesson to be learned about membership numbers, if not inclusivity.

20. The parish as a whole and in particular ministries such as Teen Life, the Altar Society, the Liturgy Committee, the Sacred Heart League and more have many opportunities to practice social justice throughout the year through food collections in Advent and Lent, diaper collections, used or new clothing collections, toiletries, blankets, or other needs. The parish is generous and these events are a success. Yet we could still do more. Hunger has no season. I would like to see a more sustained effort in this area through the Altar Society. For the last three years we have collected bags of food at the nine meetings and the retreat. In the last six months the number of bags brought to the meeting has been waning. It is easy to let things go and that is fine if the society so chooses. Yet it seems this generous act is needed more than ever. Although it was not listed as a society dream that may not have been in the forefront of the members' minds at the time of the survey. Personally, and as the President, I will continue to nourish that dream. Sometimes all it takes is a reminder.

21. I would like to see an effort by the new priests, staff, and ministerial heads to get to know the Altar Society as a group in formal and informal ways. They would be welcome to come to a meeting and meet the members personally as well. The Basilica is a rich training ground for new priests who are given their own parishes in one to two years after ordination. Learning about how a strong and viable Altar Society works can help the new pastor have strong allies in the women and assist them in their many responsibilities at their new parish.

22. We should learn from and share with other Altar Societies. We can invite them to our meetings, retreats, or a social function to keep this valuable church institution alive.

23. To help prepare potential leaders for their roles in the parish and the Altar Society in particular, a welcome brochure can be an effective tool along with a personal invitation to leadership and membership. Through our example in decoration with a beautiful flower, a moment of reconciliation, or a heartfelt conversation, these activities can capture the imagination of a person such that they want to be part of the church in the ministry of the St. Francis Altar Society. I believe that they will learn a lot from reading this book.

24. We need to rededicate ourselves to the decorative aspects of the church. As the President who appoints the Flower Committee I have created a three-team structure to distribute the workload and to decorate at Christmas, Easter, and Ordinary Time. The membership is small but adequate, reliable, and committed.

Over the years, at our retreats, we would wash or anoint each other's hands at the foot of the altar and pray a psalm that has guided the society. "May the favor of the Lord our God be ours. Prosper the work of our hands! Prosper the work of our hands!" (Psa 90:17)Perhaps this sums up our dreams as well. To survive and prosper we are invited to wake up and dream! Can we hear that voice?

Figure 29 Spiritual Development Committee, 1960

Left to right

Mrs. George White, Mrs. Frank McCulloch, Mrs. Ralph Moen, Miss Lala Ortiz, Miss Margaret Scheur and seated Mrs. Dale Miller

13

Organizational Templates and Forms

The Threads that Bind

"JUST AS NO SUBATOMIC PARTICLE EXISTS INDEPENDENT OF ITS PARTICIPATION WITH OTHER PARTICLES, SO TOO IS ORGANIZATIONAL LIFE CONNECTED."

Margaret Wheatley, modern organizational expert, 2006

ORGANIZATIONAL THEORIES

ESSENTIALLY FOR AN ORGANIZATION to be successful and sustainable it requires five things—a mission, leadership, membership, commitment and organization. As we have seen in the previous chapters the St. Francis Altar Society has had all five. Never underestimate the importance of structure for an organization to operate and endure. There needs to be a structure that is transparent, orderly, and that members can understand. Much like nature and people organizations are living matrices and they must change in order to survive and mature.

Leaders are essential in the realization of a group or organization's goals. A reflection on leadership and management modes in actual practice provides us with tested information from the real world on their differences and whether they do indeed achieve the goal of the organization they were designed to meet.

While at first glance most management styles may seen to favor efficiency and effectiveness, and for the most part these are at least assumed operational principles, on a much deeper level, management styles are a hermeneutic for the way a person and indeed humanity's richness is captured. Various models of organizational theory have developed over time, especially in the field of industrial engineering that dealt with the interface of technology, productivity, and the worker or volunteer. Many have fundamental philosophical differences that are predicated on their view of the human person.

Some saw the person as a machine whose worth was measured in efficiency and productivity. The classical model of management wants to get things done and that makes sense. In general, it is probably a unilateral method of management where directives are given from the top down. If a model can do that and still recognize the people who are the ones who do it, and can treat them with dignity and respect, it is a model that can work. Many times such models use positive reinforcement mechanisms to encourage personal development and best, albeit perhaps from a productivity point of view.In contrast to this model a communal leadership paradigm has more a more personal, relational perspective to getting things done. They may be more adept at tapping into the enthusiasm, creativity, vision and talents of the whole group. While some type of productivity on any issue stills remains the goal, the primary difference in these organizational models is how the task gets done. It may take longer to evoke those talents, but the willingness to be receptive, to listen, to accommodate, to share decision making, and knowledge with genuine interest helps to shoulder the work and offers the participants a way to work together ensconced in a philosophy of community that in many ways is Christological.

Both styles have the power to do things; the question is how is that power enacted. On the other hand, it is possible that a group, such as the church or any other organization, can fuse these models creatively for the good of the group and the organizational goals. At lease within a church style *communio*, love is the way to accomplish the goals of the group. This may take some major organization, accomplished by smaller groups, in other words, the emphasis is not only to get the task done but the shift is made that the way to do it is more or at least equally important. The work will get done by people who are whole, with all their apparent strengths and weakness. The pace of accomplishment may be slower but the methodology may be infinitely more enriching as human bonds of charity are established between hearts and minds in the living matrix of the world that we could call the body of Christ.

Modern day organizational theories reject these assumptions and stress the interconnectedness of people, their dignity, and their need for meaning and identification with work or a mission over productivity. That meaning can be obtained through membership in an organized structure. Margaret Wheatley, modern organizational expert observes, "Just as no subatomic particle exists independent of its participation with other particles, so too is organizational life connected."[1] These theories hold true as well for a religious institution such as the St. Francis Altar Society.

If one thing is evident in perusing the documents of the society is that they were organized! The society used parliamentary procedure at their meetings from day one to the present. This feature has organized the work of the society and allowed for orderly and understandable participation and interaction.

Strong organizational skills on the part of the President, followed by that of the officers, have always been the benchmark of the St. Francis Altar Society. That organization is characterized by a methodology. This combination of skills coupled with the dedication of the members makes for a solid infrastructure for any altar society. Much of the structure can be achieved through the use of forms, in many ways the physical threads that bind the work into a living nexus of service.

Forms

This chapter includes several helpful prototype documents that might assist your current altar society, or if you are planning on forming an altar society in order to lay a strong foundation for a ministry. They can also be modified for other lay ministries. The forms as templates are a way in which to structure work. However, as the previous chapters indicate, the intangible yet palpable spirit of a society or ministry is something you will need to cultivate. Each of these forms used by the St. Francis Altar Society is briefly introduced here. We hope that these forms assist you in meeting your mission! The documents are included herein.

1. Wheatley, *Leadership*, 45.

- The society's Constitution and By-Laws

  Your altar society should have a Constitution and By-Laws. Take the time to determine the mission of the society. Is it care of the church, and in what capacity? i.e. heavy cleaning or light dusting? Is it custody of the flowers or will you work with parish staff and other ministries? Who can join?Are there different types of members?What is your membership fee? What committees will help distribute your workload? When will you meet? Do you have a patron saint? What is the name of the society? Do you have any special colors or symbols to represent the society?How are things voted upon and/or amended?

- Officers' Duties

  Who are the officers of the society? What do they do?How are they selected? What are their terms of office?Delineate a clear job description and list of duties.

- Installation of Officers and Ceremony

  Adopt a protocol for installing the officers.

- Sample Agenda

  Prepare the agenda prior to the meeting and distribute at the meeting. Use the same format at every meeting. Follow standard parliamentary procedure in the meeting.

- New Membership Application

  Solicit new membership at periodic intervals. Have a new membership application with the data you need such as basic identifying information. Revise that form yearly. What are the membership dues? What does the money go towards?

- Membership Renewal Application

  If useful, have members update their personal information yearly i.e. email, phone number, etc.

- Membership Questionnaire

  If studying the organization or evaluating it in some respect, it is helpful to devise a membership questionnaire. Analyze the data collected and act on it through bringing the information collected to a subcommittee or the general membership. Evaluation is meaningless without action. Act on data.

- Retreat Planning Worksheet

  If planning a retreat, form a retreat subcommittee to outline the basic structure and features of the retreat. Then present to the membership for modification and adoption.

- Bulletin Insert

  Let your parish know what you are doing in a church bulletin insert. This can be informational such as when your retreat is being held, who is invited, what your mission is, and the accomplishments of the society. Visibility is important. Have Masses published that are said for recently deceased members or those who are ill. Regularly have Masses said for Living and Deceased members of the society, perhaps on the anniversary of the society.

- Hostess Schedule

  Plan your refreshments for each meeting with members providing refreshments on an alternating basis.

- Care of the Sacred Linens

  If your society cares for the sacred linens there are very specific ways they must be cared for, washed, ironed, folded and put when soiled. Have members who like that task sign up to do linens, perhaps on a monthly basis. Inventory linens periodically and inspect them for wear or stains and replace as needed. Make sure your linen sacristy always has plenty of linens for all liturgies.

- Church Cleaning Instructions and Cleaning Check Off List

  For those who choose to clean, if your society does this, it is important to have clear instructions on what needs cleaning, when, and how to do including cleaning products that can and should not be used. Have a team work together on weekly cleaning. A check off list and sign in sheet can help monitor the tasks.

There are many more sign up sheets that you may need throughout the calendar year. Create your own and use them to organize work, solidify plans, and elicit membership participation.

Finally, as a tasty treat, the meat portion of a meal that we served at many functions over the years, which the ladies cooked from scratch, is the famous Brisket a la Hermine Quintana. Enjoy!

Constitution and By-Laws of the St. Francis Altar Society of the Cathedral Basilica of St. Francis of Assisi, Santa Fe, New Mexico

1. Article I—Name
    1. The name of this organization shall be the St. Francis Altar Society of the Cathedral Basilica of St. Francis of Assisi.
    2. Its colors shall be brown, white, and green in honor of St. Francis.
    3. Its motto shall be "The work of the altar should be a labor of love."
2. Article II—Mission
    1. The primary purpose of the society shall be the care of the altars and sanctuary and their needs; to make our total church environment hospitable and fit for worship; to promote the personal sanctification of the members through participation in special liturgical celebrations and processions, and to observe First Friday Adoration of the Blessed Sacrament. The secondary purpose is to promote sociability among our parish community by lending assistance with pastoral projects and social events.
3. Article III—Membership
    1. Membership may be enjoyed by any person of the Cathedral Parish upon application and payment of annual dues. There are four types of membership:
    2. Regular membership
    3. Inactive membership—those members who support the Society with prayers, donations, payment of dues, telephone calling, but cannot otherwise be active.
    4. Honorary membership—those members, having been active at least 10 years, who have become inactive because of long-term illness. Payment of dues is waived.
    5. Honorary membership by invitation—members of the clergy who work with the Society but are not active members. Payment of dues is waived.
4. Article IV—Officers

1. The officers of the St. Francis Altar Society shall be: President, Vice President, Secretary, Treasurer, Past President and Spiritual Director.
2. The terms of office in this society shall be for two years. No member may hold the same office for more than two consecutive terms. However, a waiver to hold office for more than two years can be accepted and voted upon during regular elections.
3. Annual election of officers whose terms will expire shall be held at the November meeting. A majority vote, or 51 percent of the members present, is sufficient for the election of any member to office.
4. Vacancies occurring in any office shall be filled by the Executive Board until the next regular meeting.
5. The Executive Board is composed of officers of the Society and the Past President and four members constitute a quorum.

5. Article V—Meetings
    1. The Society shall hold meetings on the third Wednesday of every month, except in August and December. The President, under certain circumstances, may change the meeting date(s) for a specific reason with the consent of the Board.
6. Article VI—Parliamentary Procedure
    1. Robert's Rules of Order shall govern the Society in all cases in which they are applicable and consistent with the Constitution and By-Laws.

By-Laws

1. Article I—Nominations
    1. The President shall appoint a Nominating Committee of three members at the October meeting. This Nominating Committee shall compile a slate containing the names of paid-up members who consent to be considered as candidates for any office being vacated. The slate of officers will be voted on at the November meeting and assume their duties in January.

2. Article II—Duties of Officers
    1. The President shall be Chairman of the Executive Board; shall preside over all meetings of the Society and of the Executive Board; shall appoint all Standing Committee Chairmen; and shall be a member ex-officio of all Committees except the Nominating Committee.
    2. The Vice President, in the absence of the President, shall assume the duties of the President and shall also be Chairman of the Membership Committee. The Vice President shall also be responsible for contacting host/hostesses for monthly meetings.
    3. The Secretary shall keep the records of all meetings of the society and of the Executive Board and carry out all correspondence of the Society.
    4. The Treasurer shall be the custodian of all funds of the Society. The Treasurer shall receive all dues and make all disbursements; shall present, at regular meetings, an accurate financial account of all moneys received and expended. She/he shall furnish full statements of the financial condition of the Society. She/he shall mail statements of dues for the current year to all members following the January meeting. She/he shall maintain active membership list and forward copy to President and Secretary. The Treasurer shall be Chairman of the Ways and Means Committee.
    5. The Past President shall instruct officers and committee Chairmen of their duties and responsibilities. She/he shall assist the President in the transition of duties to maintain continuity of Society functions as a whole. She/he shall prepare the yearly calendar of Parish events that concern the Society and provide copy to the Parish Office.
    6. The Spiritual Director shall be the Rector/Pastor of St. Francis Cathedral or a representative appointed by him and shall approve membership applicants.
3. Article III—Standing Committees

    The Standing Committees of this Society shall be: (1) Altar and Sanctuary (2) Ways and Means, (3) Membership, (4) Flower, and (5) Telephone.

Standing Committee Chairpersons shall have the option to recruit up to four members from the membership at large to assist them in carrying out the duties of their respective committees.

1. The Altar and Sanctuary Committee is to schedule the care for the Altars and Sanctuary of St. Francis Cathedral. The Chairman shall be responsible for: Maintaining yearly cleaning schedule and coordinating the supply of baptismal garments with the Parish office. She/he will coordinate with the membership the buying of material, cutting and embroidering of these garments to maintain an adequate supply during the year.

2. Ways and Means Committee shall be responsible for all fund raising projects, including annual silver tea and coordinating special collections for altar flower/sanctuary needs.

3. The Membership Committee shall promote the growth and order of the society, together with all members. The committee shall receive and file applications for membership and constantly endeavor to increase same, provide new members with new member packet, which includes the Constitution, By-Laws, Membership List, Sanctuary Cleaning Instructions, Yearly Calendar and Hostess Schedule. The Committee shall provide a copy of the membership roster to the Parish Office.

4. The Flower Committee Chairperson shall be appointed by the President. The Committee shall coordinate the seasonal decorations to be used in church. This Committee shall work closely with the Parish's Liturgy Committee and Art and Environment Committee so that the Church environment contributes to a climate of hospitality that leads the Parish Community to participation in the liturgy.

5. The Telephone Committee shall be appointed by the President. The Committee shall be comprised of a Chairperson and an adequate number of calling captains who are responsible for informing members of meetings and important upcoming events.

The President shall appoint a Historian who shall take care of all books, documents and official papers that belong to the Society. These files are to be maintained and catalogued chronologically and placed in such an order that they can be within easy recall by the members.

4. Article IV—Meetings
    1. The Society shall hold meetings on the third Wednesday of the month at 1:30 p.m.
5. Article V—Finances
    1. Annual dues of the Society shall be twenty-five ($25.00) dollars and payable in January. No member shall be considered delinquent unless in arrears for twelve (12) months without sufficient reason.
6. Article VI—Benefits
    1. Members will be entitled to the offering of a published Mass at St. Francis Cathedral in the event of their death. This will also include husband/wife, parents and children of the member. All other masses will be unpublished and offered at the Carmelite Monastery. The Treasurer will pay for these Massses with Society Treasury funds.
    2. The recitation of the Rosary shall take place for a deceased member and/or a deceased member's immediate family before the funeral when the member or family request. Members, whenever possible, should attend rosaries and masses of the deceased.
7. Article VII—Amendments
    1. The Constitution and By-Laws of this Society may be amended, altered, repealed and new ones adopted by a 51 percent vote of those members present at any regular or special meeting, provided that the proposed amendment has been read at one previous regular meeting.
    2. We certify the foregoing to be a true copy of the Constitution and By-Laws duly amended and adopted by the members of this Society on the 15 day of November 2017.

Constitution/By-Laws Committee

President

Altar and Sanctuary Commmittee (Member)

Past President, (Constitution/By-Laws Special Committee Chairperson)

St. Francis Altar Society Officer Duties

Past President

1. Shall instruct officers and committee Chairmen of their duties and responsibilities.
2. Shall assist the President in the transition of duties to maintain continuity of Society functions as a whole.

President

1. Shall appoint a Nominating Committee of three members at the September/October meeting and to bring the slate to the November meeting for election of officers.
2. Shall be the Chairman of the Executive Board.
3. Shall preside over all meetings of the Society and the Executive Board.
4. Shall set the agenda of the meetings.
5. Shall appoint all Standing Committee Chairmen.
6. Shall be a member ex-officio of all committees except the Nominating Committee.
7. Shall appoint a Historian who shall take care of all books, documents, and official papers that belong to the Society.
8. May make Executive Decisions with the Board for up to $100.
9. Shall represent the Society at the Parish Liturgical Committee as well as subcommittee meetings.
10. Shall retrieve mail from Parish office.
11. Shall notify Parish Office of dates of monthly meetings for scheduling of Crispin Hall and Meeting Room dates.
12. Shall prepare the yearly calendar of Parish events that concern the Society and provide copy to the Parish Office.

Vice President

1. In the absence of the President, shall assume the duties of the President.

2. Shall also be Chairman of the Membership Committee, i.e. heads up telephone captains and calls them as needed.
3. Shall be responsible for contacting host/hostesses for monthly meetings and maintain the hostess schedule.
4. Calls captains for other information to go to the membership.

Secretary

1. Shall keep records of all meetings of the Society and the Executive Board.
2. Shall carry out all correspondence of the Society.
3. Shall submit amended minutes to President and file within one week of last meeting.
4. Shall submit minutes for upcoming meeting to President one week prior to subsequent meeting for review, agenda preparation, and meeting packets.
5. Shall maintain attendance list at all meetings (sign in people who are late).

Treasurer

1. Shall be the custodian of all funds of the Society.
    1. Shall receive all dues and make all disbursements.
    2. Shall present at regular meetings an accurate financial account of all moneys received and expended.
    3. Shall furnish full statements of the financial condition of the Society.
    4. Shall mail statements of dues for the current year to all members following the January meeting.
    5. Shall maintain an active membership list and forward copy to President and Secretary.
    6. Shall be Chairman of the Ways and Means Committee.

Installation of Officers

"Just One Little Candle"

Hand out candles to all members present. Turn off all lights. Outgoing President or installing officer says:

As we inaugurate a new year for the St. Francis Altar Society, let us begin as our Holy Mother, the Church does at Easter —with a clear, bright light shining in the darkness. Let this light represent the enthusiasm and interest of our new officers. May it shine brightly and be a foreteller of the good things to come.

Borrowing the theme of the Great Christopher Movement, that you can change the world by lighting just one little candle in the darkness, I wish to extend to ____________________ this lighted candle, a symbol of her office as President and our leader. ____________________ will you take this light, and lead us along the path set out for us by Christ, the light of the world?(Hand her lighted holy candle.)

In accepting this illumination, ____________________, you are duly installed as President of the St. Francis Altar Society.

(Hand unlighted smaller blessed candle to each officer as you address her.)

Vice President:____________________, the light you bear will increase and augment that of our President. Will you light this candle from that of our President to symbolize your acceptance of the office of Vice President?

Secretary:____________________, the light that you will shine before us will be a permanent record of the illumination of God's will accomplished by our society. Will you lessen the darkness by lighting your candle from our President's to symbolize your acceptance of the office of Secretary?

Treasurer:____________________, your candle may dwindle, but it must never go out. Will you show your willingness to accept the office of Treasurer by lighting your candle from that of our President?

The darkness in the room has lessened, but it is still not bright. Will the officers show their willingness to lead by giving of their brilliance to all members, that each of us may hold up our candle as evidence of our promise to cooperate as members of the St. Francis Altar Society?

(Officers go among members and light the small candles —members stand.)

Now, with the light of our devotion to God's will and his work before us, the spirit of the St. Francis Altar Society is aflame with a bright light. Let us pray that God will bless us and our work.

Prayer:In the name of the Father, and of the Son, and of the Holy Spirit. Amen.

Oh, Christ, who art the light of the world, help us to bear high the torch of our faith; to keep bright the flame of our love for you; to show forth the illumination of God's work as done by women; to keep alive the fire of our desire to work together to accomplish the aims of our society. Dear Mother Mary, help us to carry on thy Son's light in the darkness of this world. Let our lights so shine that the little world of our own parish will be changed for the greater honor and glory of God. Amen.

Turn lights on.

The Cathedral Basilica of St. Francis of Assisi

Altar Society Meeting Agenda

Date:

1. Call to order
2. Opening prayer of the St. Francis Altar Society
3. Welcome; Attendance sheet circulation
4. Approval of agenda
5. Secretary
    a. Reading and approval of minutes
    b. Reading of correspondence
    c. Members and family to remember in prayer and Mass
6. Treasurer's Report
7. Committee reports
    a. Altar and Sanctuary: cleaning and linen assignments
    b. Adoration attendance: Adoration flowers for the month, thanks to those from last month and providers for the next month

    c. Hostesses today thanks to and hostesses for next meeting
    d. Pastoral Council Report
    e. Liturgy Committee Report
8. Old Business
    a. Travelling Francis
    b. Any
9. New Business
    a. Any
10. Announcements
11. Closing prayer and adjournment

Membership Letter

St. Francis Altar Society of the Cathedral Basilica of St. Francis of Assisi

Since 1921 + A labor of love for the glory of God

January 2018

Dear Members of the St. Francis Altar Society,

Firstly, let me extend New Year's greetings to you on behalf of the St. Francis Altar Society of the Cathedral Basilica St. Francis of Assisi and thank you for a special 2017. Now it is time to refresh your involvement with us through your continued participation at our meetings, helping with the cleaning the church, care of the sacred linens, hostessing events, and assisting us to grow in the service of St. Francis. Our Flower Committee is renewed, growing, and the flowers need your care. We have wonderful annual retreats every summer that begin with Mass, followed by sharing in healthy food, rich friendships, and spiritual reflections. If you haven't joined us in a while let us welcome you back!

You can continue to support us in these ways and by renewing your membership fee that has increased to $25.00 to meet the society's needs in service to the parish. Dues can be brought to our meeting, the third Wednesday of every month, at 1:30 in Crispin Hall, or left at the Parish Office, or mailed to the parish. When coming to the monthly meetings, please don't forget to bring your bag of canned goods to support the St. Vincent de Paul store and our dedication to feeding the hungry.

Just a few updates+

- We have beautiful new membership ribbons that we wear to all events. They can be purchased for $10.
- Our newly designed banner continues to honor St. Francis of Assisi in the traditional colors of brown and white with the new dimension of green to celebrate Francis as the Patron Saint of Ecology and our beautiful planet wherein we do our work.
- Our one-hundred-year history book, *Wildflowers and the Call to the Altar: Mission and History of an Altar Society,* is half written by the Spiritual Development and Writing Club. We will complete it this year so it can go to press in 2019 in time to sell and to celebrate our 100th anniversary in 2021!
- New gifts for the sanctuary continue to be purchased every year from the sanctuary envelope collection.

Hope you will join us this year at our meetings or by supporting us in any way you can.
In gratitude for all you do and Happy, Blessed New Year.

Skya Abbate, President, 2005–2018

131 Cathedral Place, Santa Fe, NM 87501
phone #, email

Membership Renewal Form

St. Francis Altar Society
131 Cathedral Place
Santa Fe, New Mexico 87501

2018 Calendar Year
Name:
Address:
City and Zip Code:
Telephone Number:

E-mail: ____

Kindly return your renewal form, together with your membership dues, to the President or Treasurer at the above address or bring with you to our next meeting.

St. Francis Altar Society Questionnaire 2017

Dear Members,

As you might know, The Spiritual Development and Writing Club of the St. Francis Altar Society is writing our 100 yr. history!We would greatly appreciate it if you would fill out this questionnaire to share your experiences with us. Please fill out this form and return to _____. Please return this no later than ____ for this data to be anonymously summarized in the book. A complimentary stamp is enclosed. Your contribution of an envelope will help us keep costs down. Thank you for all you do to assist the Altar Society in its vital parish mission.

Name (optional): ________________________________

Directions: Circle or fill in your answer.

1. How long have you been in the St. Francis Altar Society?
    a. 1–5 yrs.
    b. 6–10 yrs.
    c. 11–15 yrs.
    d. 16–20 yrs.
    e. Specify other___________________________________
2. Marital Status
    a. Married
    b. Widowed
    c. Divorced
    d. Single
3. Occupation: ____
4. Age: _______

5. Educational level
   a. Less than high school
   b. Graduated from high school
   c. AA, BA, or BS College degree
   d. Masters degree
   e. Doctoral degree
6. Race/Ethnicity: choose all that apply
   a. Hispanic
   b. Native American
   c. Caucasian
   d. Specify other___________________________________
7. Have you ever been a member of any other Altar Society?
   a. Yes
   b. No
8. Have you ever been an officer of the Altar Society? If yes, circle all that apply.
   a. President
   b. Vice President
   c. Treasurer
   d. Secretary
9. Are you currently a member of any other ministry? If yes, circle all that apply.
   a. Pastoral Council rep
   b. Liturgy Committee rep
   c. Adult server
   d. Reader
   e. Extraordinary Minister of Holy Communion
   f. Treasures of Wisdom
   g. Vincent de Paul
   h. Choir

i. Martha's ministry

j. Specify other________________________________

10. What do you currently do in the Altar Society? Circle all that apply.

a. Attend monthly meetings

b. Pay membership dues

c. Clean the church monthly

d. Care for the linens

e. Seasonal decoration

f. Call members about meetings

g. Participate in Blessed Sacrament Adoration

h. Processing throughout the year

i. Specify other ________________________________

11. If you do not participate in any of these activities, why not?

____

____

____

12. What do you think is/are the most important function(s) of the Altar Society? Choose all that apply.

a. Care for the altar and the linens

b. Blessed Sacrament Adoration

c. Prayer for the ill of our family and friends

d. Hostessing parish events

e. Specify other: ________________________________

13. What do you think we could do better?

____

____

____

14. How important do you think the Altar Society is to the life of the parish?

a. Very important

b. Somewhat important

c. Not very important

d. Don't know

15. Have you ever received the St. Francis of Assisi Award from the parish? Yes/No

16. Do you think that not having a Spiritual Director has negatively affected the spirit of the Altar Society? If yes, explain how. If no, explain why not.

___

___

___

17. Do you think it is useful to know the history of your society? If yes, why and if not why not?

___

___

___

18. What do you recall as the most difficult time (s) for the St. Francis Altar Society if any?

___

___

___

19. What would you like to see the Altar Society achieve in the next 3–5 years?

___

___

___

___

___

___

20. What is your dream for the future of the St. Francis Altar Society?

___

___

___

Thank you for your participation in this survey and the St. Francis Altar Society!

St. Francis Altar Society: Retreat Planning Sheet

Committee:

Date:

Retreat talk:

Location:

Theme:

Contents:

Mass:

Presider:

Server and mass set up:

Communion ministers:

Flowers:

Gift bearers and intentions:

General Intercessions:

Music:

Handwashing/Psalm

Prayers-Altar Society Prayer

Lunch:

Phone calls:

Bulletin announcement and program:

Bulletin Insert

St. Francis Altar Society of the Cathedral Basilica of St. Francis of Assisi
Since 1921 + A labor of love for the glory of God
During Lent we are not only invited to accompany Jesus in his passion but to enter into greater discipleship. That discipleship can be well expressed in the church through ministerial involvement.

The St. Francis Altar Society invites you to join us in our ministry of service to the altar through cleaning, laundering the holy linens, adoring the Blessed Sacrament, hostessing many parish events, and promoting peace and social justice through monthly food donations to the St. Vincent de Paul store and others. This Lent become a member of the St. Francs Altar Society. Our next meeting is March 20, 2018 at 1:30–3pm in Crispin Hall. See us there as we celebrate 97 years strong of service to the altar or support us in prayer and membership dues.

Yes, I would like to become a member of the St. Francis Altar Society of the Cathedral Basilica of St. Francis of Assisi

Name____
Address____
City_____________________________________
Zip code_________________
Phone/email____

Mail this form and your $25 membership dues to the church or bring to our next meeting.

Altar Society Hostess Schedule

Vice President will remind hostesses. Please list name and phone number.

January 1. 2. 3.	July Retreat
February 1. 2. 3.	August 1. 2. 3.

March	September
1. 2. 3.	1. 2. 3.
April	October
1. 2. 3.	1. 2. 3.
May	November
1. 2. 3.	1. 2. 3.
June No meeting	December No meeting

Procedure for the Care of the Holy Cloths

Cathedral Basilica of St. Francis of Assisi

Types of Holy Cloths
D= definition; P= procedure for washing, and I=how to fold and iron

All soiled and wrinkled linens should be taken home, washed, ironed or folded and returned to proper drawers in the sacristy as soon as possible. If you are unable to do so, please call the Linen Chairperson. If you prefer, you may do all linens in the laundry room located next to our linen room.

An ironing board and iron are available if needed. If the large altar cloths are wrinkled and need to be pressed, a large bed sheet is available in the gray cabinet and should be placed underneath the ironing board to keep cloths from getting soiled.

Corporals:

D: A firm square of fine white linen (only made of linen), that is placed on the altar and upon which the vessels for the sacred species are placed

P: All corporals and purificators should be soaked in a pan of water in order to remove the wine residue (precious blood). After having done this you must wring them out and throw the water in the dirt outside (not in your sink) or pour into the sacrarium in the priest sacristy

I: Iron in threes, heavy starch

Priest Purificator

D: Oblong linen with a cross in the center. It is placed over the chalice and used by the celebrant to wipe the chalice and ciborium (ia) and purify them. They are folded twice and shaped into the form of the letter "M". They have a red trimming and a cross in center

Extraordinary Ministers of Holy Communion Purificator

D: Used to clean the cup between each person receiving the precious blood

P: Wash by hand. The washing water, which may be in contact with the sacred species, may be reverently disposed of to water the plants in the church or the earth outside one's home or pour into the sacrarium in the priest sacristy

They are folded twice and folded in center when ironed.

I: Use starch when ironing

Lavabos (finger towels)terry cloth, ideally 100 percent cotton for absorption with a cross on the bottom center

D: Finger towel used by priests to wash fingers during Mass

P: Can wash in washing machine but do not mix with other items

I: No starch, no iron. They are folded twice and center folded

Altar cloths

D: The large cloths used on top of Main Altar and the Altar in the Blessed Sacrament Chapel

P: Wash

I: Iron and starch

For problems, questions contact Chair of the Altar and Sanctuary Committee or President

Cleaning Instructions and Checklist

St. Francis Altar Society

Cleaning should be done on Friday or Saturday (day and time you and your partner prefer). Also, you should check church bulletin or call the office to inquire regarding celebrations, feast days, weddings, funerals, etc. that might be taking place so you can schedule your time accordingly. 9:00 am is a good starting time for Saturdays or you may prefer Friday morning or afternoon.

Check off that these areas were cleaned.

Dusting and Cleaning

- Sanctuary Main Altar, put spray furniture polish on dust cloth only
- Credence table (where vessels are placed for Mass)
- All chairs, kneelers, candle stands, ambo stand, lectern hymnal and directional stands
- Our Lady's Chapel (*La Conquistadora)*Prayer Request Table
- Baptismal Font: Paschal Candle stand and Ambry (where Sacramental Oils are stored).
- St. Joseph Chapel
- All the Sanctuary area
- Gift table by the baptismal fonts: Used for placing the gifts to be taken to the Altar during Mass
- Confessionals, once per month
- Archbishops' Memorial Altar Next to St. Joseph Chapel
- Main Sacristy, Minister's Sacristy, Altar Society Sacristy
- Dust all doors. Clean counters and sinks. All soiled towels should be replaced. Empty all wastebaskets. Cleaning cloths should be discarded or taken home and washed

- Tabernacle in hallway, replace linens if necessary
- Care of holy water fonts:holy water fonts must be cleaned and refilled. Empty all used holy water in the special sink with cover in the priests' sacristy. Clean and replenish all fonts with clean holy water from the font in sacristy hallway or baptismal font. Fill fonts only three quarters full to avoid spilling of water on the floor. Even if you see that fonts have holy water, they must be emptied and refilled since it has sat there for a whole week. There are labeled pitchers under the sink in the Altar Society Sacristy for use in emptying and filling the fonts
- Flowers, please water all flowers that are in need of it. If flowers or plants appear wilted throw them away. Reminder:No flowers on any altars or throughout the church during the Lenten or Advent season
- St. Anthony's Chapel, clean and dust thoroughly, including the docent's desk at entryway to the main church
- Cleaning supplies, please notify the Treasurer when cleaning supplies are running low

My sincere thanks to members who give of themselves to clean the house of the Lord. May God reward you with many blessings. Thank you.

Brisket a la Hermine Quintana

Flatcut and trimmed brisket 9x13 inch pan

Two sheets of tin foil plus two packages of Lipton onion soup mix

Put foil in pan and brisket on the foil. Sprinkle dry Lipton onion soup mix on the brisket. Seal the brisket in the foil; be sure the seal is tight so the juices don't escape as it cooks.

Bake at 300 degrees for 4–5 hours. Remove from oven and let cool in the foil for about 1 hour. Take meat out of foil and using a sharp knife, cut the meat on the diagonal into thin slices. Put sliced meat into 9x13 pan. Pour juice over meat.

Figure 30 Embracing the Future

10TH ANNUAL RETREAT PRAYER

The Call of the Altar

O holy St. Francis
Who teaches us the interconnectedness of all things
We are the lowliest of creatures
For only we can sin.
But we are elevated to be the highest
For you we can adore.
Through the joy of holy poverty
And the resurrection of the Lord
Like the birds who ate from your holy hands
We are fed with the food of eternal life.
Today we rededicate ourselves in your name
To service and the call of the altar
To rebuild God's church
In every heart and land. Amen

by Skya Abbate

14

The Future

The Call Remains the Same

"If interpretation means anything at all it must surely mean trying to understand a voice that is other than our own."

Terry Veling, theologian, 2005

In this, my final term as President of the St. Francis Altar Society, and in completing this book, concluding thoughts come to mind. This could very well be a long book if its purpose was to recount the countless gifts of charity, acts of generosity, or hours of service that the current members accomplished together never mind throughout their close to 100-year history. But overall, what I think is most important to leave behind as President and author, are the understandings derived from writing this book at a fitting juncture in the history of the society and the voice that Veling[1] refers to—that voice of the other told in this story, the voice of the call to the altar.

When I undertook the task to organize and author this book it was not that I wanted to do so! As the 100th anniversary approached, in light of the fact that all of the Altar Society documents had been passed on to me, and as the most longstanding President of fourteen years, it seemed it was a calling. Additionally, I had written my Master's thesis for my degree in Pastoral Studies and Christian Spirituality from Loyola University New

1. Veling, *Practical Theology*, 60.

Orleans on the Altar Society and my Master's degree in Sociology on voluntary organizations. I did not want to write this book alone or to tell the story only from my point of view. Thus, I proposed to the women of the Altar Society that we form a Spiritual Development and Writing Club as the mechanism for writing the history, and as a way to deepen our spirituality by learning about our faith in action. The members enthusiastically embraced the idea. Eight came forward to help write the book and you have now read the results of that group endeavor.

The world is always changing and today so many things vie for our attention. What we choose to do is a function of our priorities and our willingness to enter into discipleship. I remember when I was asked to be the President of the Altar Society in 2005 that it seemed outside the scope of my abilities and a lot of work and I already worked enough! When I mentioned that I had been nominated to be President to a parish priest he said, "It is a great privilege to serve the altar." At the time I did not understand the fullness of this statement but it was enough of a suggestion to accept the position. Even today I am sure that I do not understand the implications of this offer perhaps any more than the ladies who responded to Fr. Eligius Kunkel in 1921 but we are glad we did.

As we read the minutes and documents left to us, and as we reflected upon how to interpret the work of the Altar Society, what stands out as the common denominator of the ten decades of history of the society is the humble, faithful service to the altar and beyond, what I have coined, "the altar of the world." Through the voluminous amount of work that they performed, the members remained true to the original intent and spirit of their initial mission described in the Constitution and By-Laws and the same goals have persisted to today.

The organization of the Altar Society as a Catholic institution is declining historically as well as Mass attendance, reception of the Sacrament of Reconciliation, and participation in voluntary associations. Yet without a doubt the Altar Society has left an indelible mark upon the church, its members, and parishes. Some say the shift is because other lay ministries compete for members' attention and this may partly be true. Yet particularly in the St. Francis Altar Society members serve in multiple ministries such as Mass Coordinators, Extraordinary Ministers of Holy Communion, Readers, Treasures of Wisdom, or serve the St. Vincent de Paul store, the Pastoral Council, Martha's Ministry, the Gift Store and more. It seems more likely that women join the Altar Society as retirees who have time for participation. Many younger women have the side bets of competing jobs outside of the home, a societal trend that is understandable, and/or have young families that require their attention. But an altar society occupies a unique niche in church organization. It can offer authentic and seasoned spirituality to anyone and foremost to those who are older to serve in ministry in the house of the Lord. While times have changed, altar societies, no matter their size, fill a role that is indispensable to liturgy and parish life.

The challenges of change in the church as she too grows in holiness or falls in scandal, and the changes in rectors, ways of doing things, and membership levels will always exist. What hopefully will not change after 100 years is the society's response and fidelity to care for the altar, the preparation of the liturgical space, and its extension in cleaning and care of the holy cloths, along with the promotion of Adoration of the most Blessed Sacrament, and the fostering of parish sociability to the degree and beyond to whatever it is called to do in the name of community, peace, and social justice.

The United States Conference of Catholic Bishops in *Called and Gifted, The American Catholic Laity*, quoting *Lumen Gentium* 31 agrees and confirms that, "Not only are lay people included in God's call to holiness, but that theirs is a unique call requiring a unique response which itself is a gift of the Holy Spirit. It is characteristic that men and women hear the call to holiness in the very web of their existence" (2).[2] The Altar Society is one such web of holy service to the members and the parish gifted by the Holy Spirit.

Just as St. Francis of Assisi continues to capture the imagination of people even outside of the Roman Catholic faith 800 years after his birth, with him as our patron, it seems we should emulate his spirit of joyful poverty as we go about doing our work. In the Introduction to this book is an idea that deserves reiteration. While some say they are dying breed[3], I say Altar Societies have the opportunity to breathe life into their members and those whom they serve. The St. Francis Altar Society has shown us there is room for the holiness and fidelity of women to serve the church in every day understated ways. Under the mantle of humility, and the commitment to our mission, the women of the St. Francis Altar Society have endured like the women at the foot of the cross and blessed with the Holy Spirit bestowed in the upper room to work in the world. They have embraced the

2. USCCB, *Called.*

3. Langlois, *Parish Altar Societies.*

call to ministry and discipleship extended to all in the gospels. I am sure that such service to the altar extends beyond the church, into the world, where the reality of the love of Christ intersects with everyday life.

Laboring between heaven and earth, somewhere amidst the animals and the angels, we search for the tree of life and the pathway to God. We look for him in the myriad places the saints have treaded, in nature and books, solitude and society, prayer and liturgy, music and scripture, sacraments and contemplation. Human history is ultimately a history of spirituality, revealed in time and space, on the journey to know God. This journey is both short and long, depending upon our sense of time, but what is important is that it has begun. Such a journey is the story of the St. Francis Altar Society. Like the water that flowed from the side of Christ, the new Adam, redeeming us and making all things new, the St. Francis Altar Society, at the foot of the *Sangre de Cristo* Mountains, is a precious drop of ministerial life-giving water that nourishes the parish and others.

Those very flowers that summoned us to the society, to the altar, is the place of ultimate of reconciliation. They need to unite not divide us. The flowers insistently beckon us with the beauty and fragrance of their maker. We can share in caring for them through decorating and in watering during the most holiest of seasons when virtual gardens of poinsettias and Easter lilies thirst like us in our glorious wildflower nature for the Lord. Our service of discipleship and ministry, however imperfect, is a call initiated by Jesus "to do as I have done." It is the same voice that beckoned Francis, the same voice that summons us all to rebuild God's church. The question we pose is can you hear the call of the altar that is extended to all? We hope you can.

References

Abbate, Skya. "*Commitment and Control in a Voluntary Association*." Masters Thesis, University of Rhode Island, 1978.

———. *My Ministry Understanding and Decisions as President of the St. Francis Altar Society—Oasis of Grace in the Desert*." Masters thesis, Loyola University, New Orleans, 2012.

The American Freedom Trains Come to Pittsburgh. The Freedom Train September 1948. http://www.brooklineconnection.com/history/Facts/Freedomtrain.html

Bernier, Paul. *Ministry in the Church: A Historical and Pastoral Approach*. Mystic, CT: Twenty-Third, 1992.

Brown, Charles E. "Seward Hiltner's Contributions to Parish Ministry." *Journal of Pastoral Care*. 40 2 (June 1986) 114–118.

Dolan, Jay P., et al. "Transforming Catholic Ministry", by Joseph Henry Fichter. *Catholic Historical Review*. 77 4 (October 1, 1991) 720–722.

Dreyer, Elizabeth A. *Earth Crammed with Heaven: A Spirituality of Everyday Life*. New York: Paulist, 1994.

Dues, Greg, and Barbara Walkley. *Called to Parish Ministry: Identity, Challenges, and Spirituality of Lay Ministers*. Lima, Ohio: Academic Renewal, 2003.

Fleischer, Barbara J. "The Ministering Community Context for Religious Education: A Case Study of St. Gabriel's Catholic Parish." *Religious Education* 101 1 (Winter 2006) 104–122.

Fleischer, Barbara and Dan Gast. *Pastoral Leadership and Organization*. New Orleans: Loyola Institute for Ministry of Loyola U., 2008.

Freedom Train — Google Arts & Culture https://artsandculture.google.com/exhibit/wQqYDx49—103k

Gaffney, Ted and Terri Sortor. "Conciliation: Transforming Conflict through Faith." edited by Charles E. Zech. *The Parish Management Handbook: A Practical Guide for Pastors, Administrators, and Other Parish Leaders*. Mystic, CT: Twenty-Third, 2003.

Hawkins, Thomas. *The Learning Congregation: A New Vision of Leadership*. Louisville, KY: Westminster/John Knox, 1997.

Herbermann, Charles, ed. "Sacristan." *Catholic Encyclopedia*. New York: Robert Appleton. (1913). https://en.wikepedia.org/w/index.php?title=Altar_society&oldid=71163-0151

Hovart, Marian Therese. "*La Conquistadora* Our Country's Oldest Madonna." http://www.traditioninaction/org/religious/a008rp.htm

John Paul II. *Christifideles Laici* (*On the Vocation and the Mission of the Lay Faithful in the Church and in the World*). Encyclical. 30 Dec. 1988. *Vatican: The Holy See*. Web. http://www.vatican.va/holy_father/john_paul_ii/apost_exhortations/documents/hf_jp-ii_exh_30121988_christifideles-laici_en.html.

Langlois, Ed. "Parish Altar Societies Provide Quiet, Prayerful Service to God." *Catholic Sentinel.* 1/1/99. http://www.catholicsentinel.org/main.asp?SectionID=2&SubSectionID=35&ArticleID=3832

Lipka, Michael. "The Number of U.S. Catholics Has Grown So Why are There So Fewer Parishes." Pew Research Center. 2014. http://www.pewresearch.org/fact-tank/2014/11/06/the-number-of-u-s-catholics—has grown-sowhy-are-there-fewer-parishes/

Mazar, Peter. *To Crown the Year, Decorating the Church through the Seasons*. Chicago: Liturgy Training, 1995.

McAvoy, Jane. "The Changing Image of Parish Ministry." *Lexington Theological Quarterly,* 25 3 (1990) 65–80.

McCarty, Jacki. *The Santa Fe New Mexican*. (July 9,1989).

McCracken, Ellen. "*La Conquistadora* (Santa Fe, New Mexico)." http://lcn.chd.ucla.edu/la-conquistadora-santa-fe-new-mexico/

Nash, Gary B. *Red, White and Black. The Peoples of Early North America*. Los Angeles, 2015.

Niemier, Roch. *In the Footsteps of Francis and Clare.* Cincinnati, Ohio: St. Anthony Messenger, 2006.

The Office of the Liturgical Celebrations of the Sovereign Pontiff. The Pallium. http://www.vatican.va/news_services/liturgy/details/ns_lit_doc_20091117_pallio_en.html—11k—Nov 17, 2009 ...

Oldest State Capital—Infoplease https://www.infoplease.com/askeds/oldest-state-capita

Osborne, Kenan B. *Orders and Ministry, Leadership in the Church World.* Maryknoll, NY: Orbis, 2006.

Paul VI. *The Constitution on the Sacred Liturgy (Sacrosanctum Concilium).* Vatican Council II: The Conciliar and Post Conciliar Documents. Rev. ed. with Inclusive Language. Northport: Costello, 1996. <http://www.vatican.va/archive/hist_councils/ii_vatican_council/documents/vatii_

———. *Dogmatic Constitution on the Church,* (*Lumen Gentium*). 21 November 1964. http://www.vatican.va/archive/hist_councils/ii_vatican_council/documents/vat-ii_const_19641121_lumen-gentium_en.html

Sanchez, Joseph P. "Nicolas de Aguilar and the Jurisdiction of Salinas the Province of New Mexico, 1659–1662." *Revista Compultense de Historia de America, Servicio de Publicaciones,* Madrid: UCM 22 (1996).

Schutte, Daniel L. *Let Us Go to the Altar of God.* Hymn. OCP. (1976).

Sweetser, Thomas P. and Patricia Forster. *Transforming the Parish*. Franklin: Sheed-Rowman, 1999.

The 10 Oldest Cities in the United States—ThoughtCo https://www.thoughtco.com/oldest-cities-in-the-united-states-4144705—152k

United States Conference of Catholic Bishops. *Called and Gifted, The American Catholic Laity, Reflections of the American Bishops Commemorating on the Fifteenth Anniversary of the Issuance of the Decree on the Apostolate of the Laity*, 1998. www.usccb.org/laity/calleden.shtml

———.Committee on the Liturgy. *Built of Living Stones: Art, Architecture, and Worship. Guidelines of the National Conference of Catholic Bishops*. Nov. 16, 2000.

———.*Communities of Salt and Light: Reflections on the Social Mission of the* ...http://www.usccb.org/beliefs-and-teachings/what-we-believe/catholic-social-teaching/communities-of-salt-and-light-reflections-on-the-social-mission-of-the-parish.cfm—292k

———. *Co-Workers in the Vineyard of the Lord.* Washington, D. C., 2005.

Veling, Terry A. *Practical Theology: On Earth as it is in Heaven.* Maryknoll, NY: Orbis, 2005.

Wheatley, Margaret J. "Chaos." Pastoral Leadership and Organization. Focus Course 861. Session 10. New Orleans: Loyola Institute of Ministry of Loyola U. (2012). CD

_____. *Leadership and the New Science*, 3rd edition. San Francisco: Berret-Koehler, 2006.

Zechmeister, Gene and Jeanne Zechmeister, *The Cathedral Church of St. Francis of Assisi.* Strasbourg: France: *Editions du Signe*, 2003.

Glossary

Biscochitos: A Mexican cookie flavored with cinnamon and anise.

Cathedral: The center of the liturgical life of a diocese.

Corporal: A firm square of fine white linen upon which the vessels for the sacred species are placed.

Diocese: The center of a geographical region headed by a bishop.

Encuentro: a meeting, an encounter.

Lavabo: Terry cloth towels used by the priest to wash his hands in preparation for the consecration.

Pallium: A symbol of unity with the Pope. It is a liturgical vestment made of white wool worn over the chasuble symbolizing the bishop as the good shepherd and the Lamb crucified for the human race. The lamb's wool is meant to represent the lost, sick, or weak sheep which the shepherd places on his shoulders and carries to the waters of life.

Pastelitos: a Mexican pastry.

Peregrino: a pilgrim.

Priest Purificator: Oblong linen with a cross in the center. It is placed over the chalice and used by the celebrant to wipe the chalice and ciborium (ia) and purify them.

Extraordinary Ministers of Holy Communion Purificator: A linen used to clean the chalice between each person receiving the precious blood.

Relleno: A New Mexican green chile stuffed with cheese and deep-fried

Santos: A wooden religious statue carved in a New Mexican folk art style.

Appendix

St. Francis Altar Society Members 1975–2018

Based upon existing records. Some earlier members are included.

- Abbate, Skya
- Abeyta, Mrs. Joe
- Alba, Sofia
- Alba, Suzanne
- Albin, Sister Pauline
- Aldeis, Anita
- Aldeis, Carmela
- Anaya, Elaine
- Anaya, Helen
- Anaya, Mary
- Anchondo, Tessie
- Andreakis, Mrs. Jeanette
- Antonio, Mrs. D.
- Apodaca, Clara
- Apodaca, Rachel S.
- Archuleta, Becky
- Archuleta, Liz
- Argiro, Elisa Maria
- Armenis, Helen
- Aschenbreneau, Eva
- Atencio, Sister Emilia
- Atkinson, Laura Jean
- Atkinson, Mary Ann
- Ayala, Alicia
- Baca, Christine
- Baca, Delfina
- Baca, Margaret
- Baca, Marti
- Baca, Mary M.
- Baca, Rebecca D.
- Baines, Mrs. Jack
- Balink, Mrs.
- Balling, Mrs. Fred
- Balling, Mrs. S. A.
- Balnick, Mrs.
- Barker, Dorothy

Barker, Mrs.
Barreras, Lucy
Barrett, Eileen
Barth, Mrs.
Barton, Maria A.
Baumstack, Mrs. Theodore
Baxter, Patricia D.
Beachem, Mrs. William
Beck, Catherine
Beers, Zola
Berchtold, Mrs. Clara
Bergere, Ms. Anita
Bernard, Sister Patrick Marie
Bertino, Flora M.
Bindel, Margaret
Binder, Suzette
Blatchford, Beverly
Block, Eloisa
Bloom, Mrs.
Blow, Helen
Boatright, Mrs.
Bouvier, Ms.
Boynton, Maria Isabel
Brewer, Yolanda Vigil
Brewester, Pamela
Brockwell, Mary
Brown, Lucy
Brown, Mrs.
Burch, Mrs.
Burch, Mrs. Ralph
Bustos, Eloisa
Butler, Mrs. Joseph
Byrd, Patricia
Campbell, Ruthann
Carmen, Edith M.
Carmen, Garie Le
Carpenter, Pat
Carrillo, Margie
Carrillo, Rosemary
Carlotta, Sister
Castellano, Louise B.
Castillo, Lupe
Castillo, Maria Elena
Catanach, Adele
Catanach, Lila
Catron, Mrs. C. C.
Cavanagh, Miss
C'de Baca, Mrs. Hipolito
C'de Baca, Lucille C.
Cepedes, Matilde
Chadwick, Lisa
Chambers, Marion G.
Chapman, Mrs. John W.
Chapman, Mary
Chavez, Ernestine G.
Chavez, Rose
Chavez, Theresa M.
Cheek, Lynn

Chidester, Nattie
Christopher, Teena
Church, Lucie
Cimino, Mrs. Carl
Clancy, Mrs. Lillian
Clifford, Ms. Geraldine
Coe, Doris
Conarty, Mrs. L. R.
Conway, Mrs. Thomas
Core, Mrs.
Cornish, Margaret
Cox, Mrs.
Culler, Mrs. Loretto
Cunningham, Rachel S.
Curtis, Mary K.
Curtis, Miss
Curtis, Mrs. Rose
Daniels, Gladys M.
Daugherty, Laura
Davies, Mrs. Ann
Davies, Mrs. E. P.
Dean, Mary
DeLany, Mrs. James
Delgado, Angie
De Medina, Consuelo M.
Deneweth, Sister Margaret Renee
Depold, Elizabeth
Dewar, Eileen
Digneo, Mrs. Americo
Digneo, Stella
Di Lorenzo, Mrs. Edmund
Di Lorenzo, Irene
Dinkel, Reynalda O.
Di Palma, Anne
Di Palma, Christine
Dockwiller, Marion
Doerling, Rachel
Dofflemeyer, Carmen
Donlan, Carmen M.
Donlan, Kathleen
Donlan, Theresa
Doyle, Ms. Elizabeth
Draggon, Dorothy
Draggon, Gloria
Dressman, Agnes
Duffy, Mrs. L. D.
Dunn, Mrs. Marcella
Duran, Carmen
Duran, Mary Carmen
Duran, Taffy
Duranceau-Church, Lucie
Duscol, Mrs. Frieda
Eagan, Kathryn M.
Earnest, Mrs. Howell
Earnest, Mary
Easley, Mrs.
Eckert, Mrs. Chas
Ellis, Bambie

Ellis, Bonnie
Esquibel, Ernestine (Tina)
Esquibel, Sarah
Farrelly, Catherine
Farrelly, Elizabeth
Faucett, Ruby C.
Feeny, Cathy
Felix, Aurora M.
Fernandez, Mrs. A. M.
Fernandez, Mrs. Tony
Ferrero, Mary Frances
Fidel, Christine
Fidel, Rose.
Fladung, Mrs.
Florsheim, Mrs. E. J.
Floyd, Russel Mrs.
Folks, Gertrude
Ford, Celeste
Fordham, Marcella
Foudy, Walter
Fowler, Lucille
Fox, Mary
Frank, Josephine
Frank, Mrs.
Friday, Gloria
Friday-Santistevan, Carolee
Fuigley, Mrs. Alice
Fullerton, Mrs. Reece
Gabaldon, Gabriel
Gabaldon, Sonia
Gahr, Karen
Gallegos, Julie
Gallegos, Librada
Gallegos, Lorraine
Gallegos, Rebecca
Gallegos, Roberta (Bobbie)
Gallegos, Virginia
Gant, Mrs.
Garcia, Agnes
Garcia, Beatrice
Garcia, Clorinda
Garcia, Dolores
Garcia, Mrs. Eddie
Garcia, Josina
Garcia, Julia G.
Garcia, Leontina C.
Garcia, Mabel M.
Garcia, Martha
Garcia, Mela
Garcia, Olinda
Garcia, Simona
Garcia, Teena
Garcia, Terry
Garcia, Theresa Marie
Garcia, Tillie
Garrey, Patricia
Garrity, Mrs. John
Gary, Pat

Gaunt, Jean
Gay, Mrs. Margaret
Geyer, Juan
Gilbert, Mrs. Marian
Gildea, Sister Janet
Giron, Mary Louise
Gomez, Pauline L.
Gondeck, Muriel
Gonzales, Adela
Gonzales, Carmen Ortiz
Gonzales, Cecilia T.
Gonzales, Connie
Gonzales, Mrs. Eufemia
Gonzales, Katherine
Gonzales, Lucy M.
Gonzales, Patricia G. (Pat)
Gonzales, Rita
Gonzales, Stephanie
Gonzales, Tillie V.
Gonzales-Neilson, Rosemarie
Gonzalez, Mrs. Flo
Gorman, Mela
Gormley, Mrs. L. F.
Gormley, Mrs. L. L.
Gormley, Ms. Mary
Gorneau, Sister Rita
Gough, Valerie M.
Graham, Therese
Grant, Anita
Greer, Mrs. John
Greer, Sara Jane
Grenfell, Julianne
Griego, Delfine
Gruel, Geneieve
Gubernatis, Michele
Gutierrez, Grace
Gutierrez, Grace
Gwin, Dawn
Haake, Mrs. Floyd (Elsie)
Halpin, Louise
Hampel, Irene
Hampel, Margaret
Hampel, Mrs. W. C.
Harkins, Mrs. Josephine
Hart, Flo
Hart, Mrs. J. A.
Harvey, Gloria
Harvey, Rita
Hasselwander, Ione
Heffleman, Mrs. C.
Heffelman, Mrs. Malcolm
Henning, Marion
Henry, Mrs. J. T.
Herrera, Martina
Hess, Miss Rose
Hickey, John
Hickey, Sharon
Hoessler, Elizabeth H.

Hollis, Mrs. Pat
Hollis Romero, Amelia
Holloway, Theresa
Hopson, Mrs. John
Howard, Cynthia
Hurley, Karenna
Hurley, Mrs. Mary
Hutchinson, Mrs. William
Ives, Peter
Jaeger, Mrs. Vincent
Jaramillo, Sophie
Javelona, Rose
Johnson, Candy
Johnson, Lillian
Johnson, Mrs. Lyle Quintana
Johnson, Mrs. Sam
Jones, Maurine C.
Jones, Peggy
Jones, Mrs. Ruth B.
Jones, Mrs. William
Karlson, Marian
Keeler, Grace
Keeran, Jeanette
Kelly, Jeanne W.
Kelly, Margaret
Kelly, Mrs. R. P.
Kelsey, Mrs.
Kennedy, Ann
Kennedy, Eloise
Kennedy, Mrs. John
Kenny, May
Kidder, Lillian
Kilkenny, Rita
Kleven, Concha Ortiz y Pino
Kolbe, Susan
Kollasch, Angie
Korzak, Carrie Lynn
Koury, Amada
Koury, Julia
Koury, Lucy
Kozbul, Becky
Krizman, Patricia
La Badie, Flora
La Badie, Rosina
Lang, Mary Genevieve
Langhorst, Joyce
Lanigan, Mrs. V. J.
Lawrence, Carrie
LeBlanc, Sister Shirley
Lechner, Alice
Leckner, Mrs. Thomas
Lee, Nancy Ann Valdez
Leith, Mrs. Angela
Lesko, Corrine G.
Levario, Josephine
Li, Nancy Ann
Lidel, Mrs.
Liepins, Leila

Lithgow, Gloria
Livingstone, Jane
Lloyd, Mrs. Russell
Lomax, Cathy
Longworthy, Ms. Marjory
Loomis, Dianne
Lopez, Consuelo M.
Lopez, Jessie M.
Lopez, Mrs. Lettie
Lopez, Lucy
Lopez, Margaret M.
Lucero, Louise
Lucero, Sofia V.
Ludi, Pina
Lujan, Edalia P.
Lujan Jr., Mrs. Manuel (Jean)
Lunt, Nicketti C.
Mabry, Clara
Macias, Sister Josephine
Mackel, Mary Frances
Maestas, Dolores
Magers, Mrs. Brady
Maldonado, Mrs.
Maloney, Anne
Mares, Marcelina
Mares, Mary R.
Martin, Mela
Martinez, Celine
Martinez, Christina
Martinez, Consuelo
Martinez, Estefanita
Martinez, Frances M.
Martinez, Juanita
Martinez, Maryanne
Martinez, Mary Jane
Martinez, Nena
Martinez, Rose
Martinez, Rosina R.
Martinez, Vera
Matic, Cecilia M.
May, Miss
McBride, Agnes
McBride, Mrs. R. P.
McCabe, Mrs.
McConvery, Mrs. John
McCullough, Anna
McCullough, Mrs. Frank
McDonald, Mary E.
McIntyre, Jeanelle
McIntyre, Ruth
McKinney, Frances
McKirnan, Mary Alice
McMullen, Sister Penny
McNeil, Mrs. David
McNeil, Muriel
McNeill, Mrs.
Mead, Leonor A.
Medina, Consuelo M.

Medrano, Esther
Meers, Sister Mary Elaine
Menking, Susan
Mera, Mrs. Frank
Messior, Sister Gabrielle
Meyers, Mrs. May
Miera, Adela
Milan, Kathi
Miller, Mrs. Dorothy
Miller, Mrs.
Miller, Olga
Mirabal, Amy Hart
Moehn, Clara
Moehn, Mrs. Ralph P.
Montoya, Betty
Montoya, Carrie
Montoya, Christy
Montoya, Claudia
Montoya, Della
Montoya, Elizabeth
Montoya, Lillie
Montoya, Rosa
Montoya, Rose
Moore, Marilouise
Morales, Socorro
Morgan, Mrs. A. N.
Moya, Mrs. Joseph
Moyanahan, Mrs. Brian
Moyer, Sister Mary Elizabeth
Moynahan, Frances T.
Mulligan, Mrs.
Murphy, Deidre
Murphy, Geraldine
Murphy, Joan
Murphy, Kay
Murphy, Mrs. Leo
Murphy, Mrs. May
Murski, Carol
Najaka, Maria
Najjar, Correen Mae
Newfield, Olivia
Newfield, Ruth
Nooger, Cleo C.
Norton, Helen C.
Novakovitch, Mrs. John
Ocana, Levinia (Mary)
Ocana, Libby
O'Kane, Adell
Ortega, Jo
Ortega, Sadie V.
Ortiz, Crucita
Ortiz, Dolores Duke
Ortiz, Mrs. Donacio
Ortiz, Helen C.
Ortiz, Mrs. Lala
Ortiz, Manuel
Ortiz, Rosina A.
Ortiz, Ruby S.

Ortiz, Sally B.
Ortiz, Sara
Ortiz, Sinforosa
Ortiz y Davis, Mrs. Frank
Ortiz y Pino, Concha
Ortiz y Pino, Virginia
Owens, Marilyn
Owings, Stella
Pacheco, Socorro
Padilla, Mrs. Norberto
Pell, Marjorie
Pelzel, Sister Caroline
Perez, Bertha
Perez, Lucille
Pesenti, Bernadette
Peters, Joan
Phipps, Mary Claire
Pineda, Raymond
Pinnington, Mrs.
Pitel, Patricia
Pogorski, Danuta M.
Porterfield, Frances A.
Porterfield, Mrs. Ted
Pound, Mrs.
Powell, Edith
Proebstal, Mrs. Charles
Prokosch, Cecilia
Quigley, Mrs. Alice
Quintana, Hermine
Quintana, Maria Sinfuentes
Quintana, Nancy
Ramirez, Belina
Ramirez, Louise
Ramirez, Mrs.
Read, Mrs. Myrtle
Reese, Mary
Reese, Mary Agnes
Reid, Christine
Rietman, H. Jeanne
Riggs, Margaret
Rivera, Carolina C.
Rivera, Donna
Rivera, Liza
Rivera, Maria C.
Rivera, Marie L.
Rivera, Terry
Rivera, Tillie
Robinson, Thelma N.
Rodriguez, Jean G.
Rodriguez, Leanor R.
Rodriguez, Lucilla
Rodriguez, Stella
Rogers, Margaret A.
Rogers, Vernice
Romanik, Pauline
Romero, Mrs. Albert
Romero, Ethel
Romero, Mrs. Josephine

Romero, Mary
Romero, Mary M.
Romero, Ophelia
Romero, Patricia A.
Romero, Ruby
Romero, Theresa
Rosales, Connie
Rosales, Mrs. Rudy
Rothy, Mary E.
Roybal, Donelia O.
Roybal, Felice
Roybal, Mercedes
Roybal, Mrs. Theo
Roybal, Theresa
Roybal, Mrs. Victor T.
Rucksthul, Imogene
Russel, Sister Joseph
Russel, Madge
Russel, Sister Mary Henry
Russell, Mrs. Wolcott
Ruth, Kathryn
Ryan, Tessa
Sabourin, Sister Patricia
Salazar, Erneda
Salazar, Joanne
Salazar, Louise D.
Salazar, Richard
Salazar, Sadie
Salazar Ives, Patricia
Salvati, Mrs.
Sanchez, Aurora
Sanchez, Esther
Sanchez, Lucy
Sanchez, Margaret
Sanchez, Max
Sanchez, Mrs. P. P.
Sanchez, Siiri
Sanchez, Theresa
Sanders, Kathryn
Sandoval, Margie V.
Sandoval, Socorro
Schoepke, Carl
Schubauer, Sister Pat
Schuit, LaVerne R.
Schutz, Rosina
Schweish, Mrs. Juliet
Scoggins, Mrs.
Scott, Mrs. Robert
Sedillo, Emelia
Sedillo, Sister Sylvia
Seitz, Julia
Sellars, Mrs.
Sellers, Mrs. D. K.
Sellers, Mrs. H. B.
Sellingsloh, Hulda
Sena, Mrs. Claude
Sena, Mrs. Jose
Sena, Juanita

Sena, Michael
Sena, Roseanne
Serna, Frances
Shampton, Sister Irene
Shaya, Zelma
Shehee, Mary Ellen
Sifuentes, Maria
Sifuentis, Mary
Silva, Rosina
Sisneros, Emelda
Smith, Frank
Smith, Miquela
St. Peter, Frances
Staab, Mrs. Charles C.
Staab, Margaret
Stack, Mrs. Francis (Katy)Stack,
Stark, Josephine G.
Stauffer, Mrs.
Stauffer, Virginia H.
Steimel, Leah
Stewart, Helen
Stewart, Mrs. L. B.
Stewart, Mrs. L. M.
Stiha, Elena
Stowell, Sister Phyllis
Stull, Mrs.
Stump, Lydia Mae
Stump, Martha
Sweeney, Clara
Sweeney, Mrs.
Sweeney, Mrs. R. P.
Syman, Flora
Tavelli, Celina D.
Taylor, Matianna
Teed, Margaret
Teed, Marjorie
Tennyson, Lillian K.
Thomas, Mrs.
Thompson, Mrs.
Tipton, Mrs. J. E.
Torres, Mrs. J. S.
Trainor, Mrs.
Trujillo, Ella
Trujillo, Gloria F.
Trujillo, Helen
Trujillo, Mardell
Trujillo, Margaret
Turney, Mary
Vaden, Mrs.
Vadin, Mrs. Mary
Valdez, Alfredo Mrs.
Valdez, Jenny
Valdez, Paola
Valdez, Paul A.
Valdez, Paul S.
Valdez, Teresina
Valdez, Valentina
Van Curen, Mrs. Richard

Vandenberg, Ethel
Vanden Heuvel, Mrs. P. P. Sanchez
Vandenhuvel, Mrs. G. L.
Van Der Schuren, Margaretha
Van Duskirk, Mrs. O. D.
Van Heche, Ms. Peggy
Van Hecke, Mrs. C. D.
Van Kampen, Pat
Van Worham, Mrs.
Vigil, Anna Mae
Vigil, Bernardita
Vigil, Celine
Visniski, Mrs. Mary
Von Bredow, Judith
Von Lehmden, Alice
Wallace, Helen
Wallace, Mrs. William
Walsh, Margaret
Walsh, Margaret
Walsh, Mrs. Thomas B.
Weafer, Margaret
Werner, Theresa M.
West, Josephine G.
Wheeler, Helen June
White, Mrs. George
Wicks, Virginia
Wulff, Carol
Yontz, Mrs. H. C.
Youngers, Jane
Zackner, Katherine
Ziemen, Sister Marcianna
Zimmerman, Alvina P.